956

How To Write Letters
For All Occasions

How To Write Letters For All Occasions

BUSINESS LETTERS

By Alexander L. Sheff

*Principal of Eastern Business and
Secretarial School, New York*

SOCIAL LETTERS

By Edna Ingalls

*Formerly of Miss Beard's School
and Drew Seminary*

Garden City Books

GARDEN CITY, NEW YORK

Contents

PART ONE

BUSINESS LETTERS
By Alexander L. Sheff

INTRODUCTION		3
I	MAKING YOUR LETTER ATTRACTIVE	5
	Selecting the Right Tools	5
	Your Typewriter	5
	Your Paper	6
	Your Letterhead	7
	Your Envelopes	7
	How to Use Your Tools	8
	Spacing the Typewriter Lines	8
	Width of Margins	9
	Folding the Letter	10
II	PARTS OF THE BUSINESS LETTER	11
	The Heading	11
	The Inside Address	13
	The Salutation	16
	The Body of the Letter	17
	The Complimentary Close	19

v

The Signature 20

The Outside Address 22

III THE LANGUAGE OF THE BUSINESS LETTER 23

Punctuation 23

Capitalization 31

Spelling 32

Syllabication 33

Writing Hints 33

"Business English" 36

Avoiding "Dead" Expressions 38

IV ROUTINE BUSINESS LETTERS 40

Acknowledgments 40

Stopgap Letters 46

Confirming Letters 47

Making Inquiries 48

Answering Inquiries 52

Secretarial Letters 57

V LETTERS ABOUT GOODS AND SERVICES 59

Asking for Prices and Samples 63

Ordering Goods 64

Acknowledging Orders 67

Shipments and Deliveries 69

Follow-ups 71

Bargaining Letters 71

VI LETTERS OF COMPLAINT AND ADJUSTMENT 76

Writing Letters of Complaint 76

Answering Complaints 82

VII LETTERS ABOUT CREDIT   88

To Customers Asking for Credit Information   88

Customers Giving Credit Information   91

Asking References for Credit Information   94

References Giving Credit Information   95

Granting or Refusing Credit   97

Asking for Payment in Advance   99

VIII COLLECTION LETTERS   101

Letters That Ask for Payment   102

Letters That Urge Payment   103

Letters That Insist on Payment   105

Letters That Demand Payment   107

Set of Collection Letters   109

  Wholesale   109

  Retail   111

  Professional Men and Small Traders   112

Debtors' Explanations   113

Answering Debtors' Explanations   116

Collection Sentences and Phrases   118

IX PERSONAL BUSINESS LETTERS   123

Greetings   123

Acknowledgments of Greetings   124

Letters of Congratulation   125

Letters of Sympathy   127

Letters of Introduction   128

Letters to Officials   129

  Correct Forms of Address   129

  Letter to the President of the United States   133

Letter to a Senator or Congressman   133
Letter to an Editor   134

X   LETTERS THAT SELL GOODS AND SERV-
    ICES   135
General Sales Letters   136
Follow-up Letters   149
   Sales Letters   150
   To Old Customers   151
   Salesmen's Calls   152
   Dealers' Letters   153

XI   APPLICATIONS FOR JOBS—AND REPLIES   156
Answering Advertisements   156
Letters Seeking Positions   160
Replies to Applicants   162
References and Recommendations   163
Following up References   165
Replies from References   166

PART TWO
SOCIAL LETTERS
By Edna Ingalls

INTRODUCTION   171

XII   SUGGESTIONS FOR WRITING SOCIAL LET-
    TERS   173
Forms of Address   174

XIII   INVITATIONS, ACCEPTANCES, REGRETS   177
Luncheon   177
Breakfast   179

Contents

Dinner | 180
Theater, Opera, Football Game | 186
Formal and Informal Dances | 188
Engagement | 191
    Announcement | 191
    Good Wishes and Congratulations | 192
Wedding | 196
    Formal Invitations | 196
    Informal Invitations | 198
    Recalling of Invitations | 201
    Replies to Gifts | 202
    Wedding Announcements | 203
    Wedding Anniversaries | 204
Calling Cards for Invitations | 204
Addressing Invitations | 206
Replying to Invitations | 206
School Functions | 207
Children's Parties | 209
Announcement of a Birth | 210
The Christening | 211

XIV NOTES AND REPLIES | 213
Notes of Congratulation | 213
Asking Favors | 221
Gift Notes | 223
School Excuses | 225
Notes of Apology to Neighbors | 227
A Broken Appointment | 228
Illness Notes | 229
Condolences | 232
Asking a Person to Appear on a Program | 234
The Note of Introduction | 237

Recommending a Girl for a Sorority   238

Invitation for a Short Visit   239

The Week-End and House Party   241

   Bread-and-Butter Letters   243

   Long Visits   245

XV   OTHER SOCIAL LETTERS   249

Travel   249

   Bon Voyage   251

Household Affairs   255

To the New Rector   257

Family and Intimate Friends   258

   To a Daughter Away at School   258

   The Daughter Asks for Advice   259

   From a Young Son at Camp   262

   Between School Friends   263

   Asking a Friend to Act as Chaperone   269

   Request for Information   270

   Confirmation   271

   Request for Money   272

   School Matters   273

   The Soldier   276

PART ONE

BUSINESS LETTERS

By Alexander L. Sheff
Principal of Eastern Business and Secretarial School, New York

INTRODUCTION

The first part of this book is devoted to Business Letters; the second part to Social Letters. However, the first three chapters will prove helpful to the readers of both sections, as they contain the fundamentals of all correspondence—punctuation, capitalization, and spelling—along with useful information on the tools and equipment generally used in letter writing.

The Business Letters section has been planned for men and women now in business and for those who expect to enter this field. It is for both employers and employees—for manufacturers, shopkeepers, office managers, correspondents, secretaries, and those who on occasion find it necessary to write letters to business concerns.

Chapter by chapter, this book takes up nearly every kind of business correspondence. In addition to detailed instructions, each chapter presents many sample letters to use as guides in the writing of that particular type of letter. The subjects covered include

3

routine letters of acknowledgment, inquiry, and confirmation; letters about goods and services; letters of complaint and adjustment; letters about credit and collection; sales letters; personal business letters; letters of application for positions, and replies.

Just as your speech and dress express your personality, so your letters represent you on paper. In showing you how to master correct form and clarity of expression, this volume will help you to create a good impression in your letters and to obtain the results you want. More effective business letters mean greater business success.

A. L. S.

I. MAKING YOUR LETTER ATTRACTIVE

Your business letter represents the firm you own (or work for) just as much as the personality of its salesmen and the quality of its goods or services. Therefore, you want your letters to make the best possible impression on those who receive them.

Start out with a well-running typewriter with the appropriate size of type. Be sure that the ribbon is clean so that it does not smudge or print too faintly. Use a good quality letter paper that is in keeping with the type of business you are engaged in. Make your letterhead reflect the personality of your firm, and finally, see that your envelopes match your stationery.

SELECTING THE RIGHT TOOLS

Your Typewriter

With very few exceptions, all modern business letters are written on a typewriter. The two sizes of type most generally used are pica and élite.

The pica is by far the more common and practical size of type for the average business. It is larger than the élite, and because of its size makes clearer carbon copies. However, many businesses and professions prefer the élite because of its dignified appearance.

Few business houses use both sizes of type. With the élite, you can make short letters look very attractive by writing the short way of a sheet of stationery—5½ × 8½, or 7¼ × 10½ ("Monarch" size).

As to color, black typewriter ribbons are the most commonly used for business letters. However, if you write on tinted paper you may want to use a typewriter ribbon to harmonize with it.

Since you would not send out damaged merchandise, you must not mail any damaged letters. Letters should be free from smudges, erasures and blots. Words crossed out and re-written, words added between the lines make an equally poor impression.

Your business letters should always be: neat, readable, dignified, businesslike.

When you have mastered these preliminary details, you will find it all the easier to organize the component parts of your letters and to consider the writing itself.

Your Paper

Most business firms use 8½ × 11 inch letter size paper. This is found to be the most convenient for general correspondence. Other firms, however, use letter paper that is 7¼ × 10½ inches, and a few firms use half-sheets for general correspondence, but this 5½ × 8½ inch size is more commonly used for memoranda on which only a few lines are written.

The quality of the paper should be as fine as the firm can afford. White paper is more commonly used than tinted, but businesses that wish to make a definite style impression frequently use a lightly colored paper.

Your Letterhead

Modern business letterheads are dignified and simple, in contrast to the old-fashioned letterheads that were usually very ornate, and overlong. The name of the firm, institution or individual, and the address should be placed at the top of the letterhead. The same face of type in various sizes is always good form on letterheads and envelopes. Any good printer will design and print the right kind of letterhead and envelope that will be in keeping with your business requirements.

Your Envelopes

As a general rule, envelopes should match the letterhead in color, quality and weight. A variety of sizes are available, but the most frequently used are the commercial (6¼ or 6¾ size), the large official (No. 9 or No. 10), and the legal size.

How to Use Your Tools

When you have selected the right tools, you will want to use them with the greatest of care. You could have the finest clothes in your closet yet not be well-dressed unless you kept your clothes in order and wore them at the right times. Attractiveness in letter writing is largely a matter of spacing your lines, watching your margins, neatly organizing the various elements in your letters, and folding your letters into the envelopes for the convenience of the recipients.

Spacing the Typewriter Lines

Most long letters are single-spaced, with double spaces between paragraphs. If there is a one-line subhead in the body of such a letter, a double space should be allowed before and after it.

Short letters may be double-spaced, with triple spaces between paragraphs. However, when the paragraphs are indented, double spacing between them is correct.

In a single-spaced letter, four spaces should be left between the date and the address of the recipient. Two spaces should be left between the address and the salutation ("Dear Sir" or "Dear Madam"), between the salutation and the beginning of the body of the letter, between the end of the body of the letter and the complimentary close and the typed name of the firm. Four spaces are usually left after the typed name of the firm for the writer's signature, but this space may be varied according to the size of the handwriting.

Width of Margins

Letters are bound by margins at the top and bottom, and on both sides. The width of these margins is an important factor toward the attractive appearance of all letters.

The width of the margin varies with the length of the letter. Long letters have narrow margins (top and bottom, and at the sides). Short letters have wide margins (top and bottom, and at the sides).

When the letter is long, the margin on the left side should be at least an inch wide, and the margin on the right should be approximately the same.

Top and bottom margins should be about equal in depth. Most letters have engraved or printed headings. When the letter covers a full page, the margin should begin from one to one and one-half inches below the base of the letterhead. And when there is no engraved or printed heading, or when the letter runs over to a second page, the top margin should be one and one-half inches. When the letter is shorter, the top margin can be deeper with the bottom margin correspondingly higher. The second page of a letter should have the same width of margin as the first, and the last page should, of course, have the same margins at the top and sides, but end wherever convenient.

The second page of a letter is just as important as the first, and the paper should correspond in size, quality, and color. It should be headed at the *left* with the name of the correspondent; in the *center* with the number of the page; and at the *right* with the date. In the event that the pages of the letter get separated, this data at the top helps you or your correspondent to identify them.

Under no circumstances should an ordinary business letter be continued on the *back* of a sheet. Never write on both sides of a sheet.

Folding the Letter

Letter paper should always be a trifle narrower than the length of the envelope so that the letter will fit neatly into it. The number of folds depends on the size of the envelope. The No. 10 envelope is the size most commonly used and requires that letter paper be folded the long way into three equal parts.

II. PARTS OF THE BUSINESS LETTER

The arrangement of the different parts of a business letter makes a world of difference in the impression it conveys. It is no more suitable for a letter to go out without the proper date line, salutation and other elements, than it would be for the head of a large concern to call on a client in slacks and tennis shoes. Unless a business letter follows the accepted correct form, the person receiving it may very well discredit the standing of the company that has sent it out.

The business world expects certain formalities in letters from reputable firms, and woe to the letter writer who neglects them. In the main these formalities of a business letter involve six parts:

1. Heading
2. Inside Address
3. Salutation
4. Body of the Letter
5. Complimentary Close
6. Signature

Sometimes there is a seventh part called the Postscript.

THE HEADING

Most business paper is engraved or printed with a letterhead. This gives the name of the company, and usually the address. When the address is given, the heading need consist of only the date.

Here is an example:

ROBERT C. JONES HARNESS CO.
444 Beal Street
Cleveland, Ohio

January 12, 19——

The letterhead is usually centered at the top of the sheet. When you write on paper without a letterhead, your heading should include the firm's address, and the date. This heading is written toward the upper right side of the paper. Headings may be written in either "step" or "block" form. In the step heading, each line after the first is indented beyond the preceding one.

31 Astor Place
New York, N. Y.
June 27, 19——

In the block heading, all the lines are written flush with the first one.

378 Lexington Avenue
New York, N. Y.
July 8, 19——

Occasionally social secretaries and professional studios use an unusual type of heading, such as:

> June
> 23
> 19——

To avoid the possibility of any misunderstanding on the part of the person to whom you are writing it is very important that you make the date of your letter perfectly clear. The name of the month should be spelled out in full. An abbreviation is clear enough, but it lacks distinction. And never write 10/7/42 for the date. In the first place, it gives an impression of hurriedness, and in the second place, it is easily misunderstood. Americans would read the date "October 7, 1942," but the British would read it "July 10, 1942."

The beginning of the date, and the beginning of the complimentary close, should line up.

THE INSIDE ADDRESS

The inside address contains the name and address of the firm or individual to whom you are writing. This makes a record on the carbon copy which serves to identify the letter for filing purposes.

The inside address should be in line with the left-hand margin. It should start two to four lines below the last line of the heading. Either the step or block form may be used. The block form is much quicker, because no time is lost in indenting each line.

In general, there are three kinds of addresses.

(1) To an individual in a firm:

> Mr. John J. Wiley,
> Ajax Oil Company,
> 246 Broadway,
> Oklahoma City, Okla.

(2) To an anonymous official in the firm:

> The Traffic Manager
> Benton Bolt Company
> 344 Rue Road
> Chicago, Ill.

(3) To the firm itself:

> Peter J. Rowe Hat Co.,
> 33 Lafayette Street,
> Tampico, Fla.

Sometimes another kind of address is used. A letter may be directed to the attention of a department head, but opened by anyone in the firm:

> Junior Miss Style Co.
> 444 Seventh Avenue
> New York, N. Y.

> Attention of the Advertising Manager

If you wish to address your letter to the attention of an individual, simply follow the form just given, but change the fourth line to read:

Attention of Mr. John K. Jones

"Attention of" should be centered, but two spaces should be left between the address and this line, and between this line and the salutation. The "Attention of" line may or may not be underscored.

In social and formal letters, the inside address may be written at the foot of the letter and to the left of the signature. The margin in this case is the same as it would be if the address were placed at the top.

If you prefer to punctuate the inside address, place a comma after each line except the last, which requires a period. Always place a period after abbreviations and initials.

The titles "Mr.," "Miss," "Mrs." should never be left out. Never use "Mr." with a name when you are writing "Esq." (Esquire) after it. The proper form is, "John Hammond Smith, Esq."

When writing to a woman, always address her as she signs herself. It is always considered correct to address a woman as "Miss," unless, of course, she has signed herself as "Mrs."

"Messrs." is used in addressing partners, as:

Messrs. Smythe & Weston

While American doctors and professors do not use their titles as frequently as Europeans, these titles, as well as others, should always be used in a business letter. For instance:

>Dr. Charles Brown
>Charles Brown, M.D.
>Prof. James Smith
>Rev. Harold Jones
>Hon. John Black

("Hon." is used for senators, congressmen, ambassadors, governors, judges, mayors, and heads of government departments.)

For greater formality, Prof., Rev. and Hon. should be spelled out, as follows: Professor, The Reverend, The Honorable.

Other forms of address used for government officials and church dignitaries are listed on pages 129, and 174, respectively.

THE SALUTATION

The salutation in a business letter is simply the written equivalent of "Hello" or "Good Morning." It should be written flush with the first line and two spaces below the last line of the inside address. The only punctuation needed after the salutation is the colon (:). Salutations most commonly used are:

>Dear Madam:
>Dear Sir:

> My dear Madam:
> My dear Sir:
> Gentlemen:
> Dear Sirs:
> Dear Mr. Bronson:
> My dear Mrs. Green:

Note that in the more formal "My dear Sir," the word "dear" is not capitalized. A woman, whether married or not, is addressed as "Dear Madam." If the writer is acquainted with the correspondent, the less formal "My dear Mr. Jones," or "Dear Mr. Jones," may be used. If you are writing informally to a personal business friend, address the person as "Dear Bill" or "Dear Sally."

When writing to a firm, the expression "Gentlemen" is more common than "Dear Sirs," though the latter is in perfectly good taste. Only in letters to government officials, should the formal salutations "Sir" or "Sirs" be used. When writing to a firm where employer and associates are women, the salutation should be "Mesdames."

Form or circular letters can be addressed to groups of people instead of to individuals. Common examples are:

> Dear Readers:
> Dear Soap Manufacturer:
> Dear Fellow Worker:
> Dear Customer:

Because such salutations are a little cold, many firms prefer using a personal heading in form and circular letters, as "Dear Mrs. Smith."

THE BODY OF THE LETTER

The body of the letter is the subject matter or main part of the message. Here is an example of a typical business letter, complete with Heading, Inside Address, Salutation, and Body.

> 34 Main Street,
> Johnstown, Illinois,
> August 3, 19——.

Mr. Roger G. Baldwin,
740 Dakota Street,
Billville, South Dakota.

Dear Sir:

Thank you for your letter of July 28.

We are sorry that there has been a slight delay in filling your order. As you may know, we are now working on a full 24-hour schedule, and we have found it difficult to obtain sufficient raw materials. You will be pleased, however, to know that we can definitely ship your order no later than next Thursday.

Our hope is that this has not inconvenienced you.

The actual writing of the body of the letter, and of other parts, the beginning and closing paragraphs, will be taken up in later sections of this book. Here we are dealing with the mechanics of letter writing.

The body of the letter, then, may consist of only

one paragraph, or of as many paragraphs as you need to convey your message clearly and pleasantly. When your message is a fairly long one, break it up into a number of paragraphs, each containing one major thought, for the convenience of your reader. Paragraphs may be either in block or indented form. When using the block form, the first line of each paragraph begins flush with your left-hand margin. And when using the other form, indent from five to ten spaces at the beginning of each paragraph.

It is advisable that even in a comparatively short letter separate paragraphs should be made of the beginning, the body of the letter, and the closing paragraph. This makes your message appear neater and easier to read and understand.

THE COMPLIMENTARY CLOSE

Just as the salutation is the written equivalent of "Good Morning," so the complimentary close is the written equivalent of "Good-by." "Yours truly" is one of the forms most commonly used, but there are many from which to choose:

> Yours very truly,
> Very truly yours,
> Yours respectfully,
> Yours very respectfully,
> Very respectfully yours,
> Sincerely yours,
> Yours sincerely,

Faithfully yours,
Very faithfully yours,
Yours faithfully,
Yours very faithfully,
Cordially yours,
Very cordially yours,
Yours cordially,
Yours very cordially,

The correct complimentary close is the one most appropriate for your purpose. Each implies a different degree of formality or friendship. The complimentary close should mean what it says. You would hardly write "Yours cordially" to someone you were about to sue, or "Yours respectfully" to a casual business acquaintance.

The Signature

The signature, the name of the person who wrote or dictated the letter, should always be written by hand. A rubber stamp makes a poor showing. The signature should be written legibly. It is customary for most business firms to have the signature typed first, with the name of the sender written above the typed signature, to avoid all possibilities of misunderstanding.

The name of the writer is all the signature required in a letter coming from an individual.

Yours truly,
Alfred Johnson

When the writer represents a firm, the name of the organization should be included in the signature. There are several ways of doing this.

Yours truly,

—————————————Office Manager
South Philadelphia Hat Company

Yours truly,
The Mason & Jones Company

By

Between the complimentary close and the typed signature, four spaces are usually allowed. The number of spaces left for the written signature depends on the size of the handwriting. If the firm name is used after the complimentary close, sufficient space must still be left for the handwritten signature.

If a letter is dictated, give in the lower left-hand corner the initials of the person who dictated it and the stenographer who typed it, so that it can be easily identified. This is done as follows: JP/AJ, TF:HH, LI-JR, or JTS.mb. Thus we know that John Palmer dictated to Annette Jackson, Theodore Foster to Harriet Howe, Lewis Ingraham to Jane Rumford, or John T. Smith to Mary Burns.

When we are enclosing something in a letter—a bill, notice, check, a copy of another letter, etc.—attention should be called to it by writing "Enclosure" or "Enc." If there is more than one enclosure, an "s" should be added for the plural. Type this under the initials of the person who dictated and the one who typed the letter.

THE OUTSIDE ADDRESS

The outside address which goes on the envelope follows the form of the inside address, either block or step, and should be typed on the envelope a little toward the right center. However, when the names making up the address are long, the writing should start nearer the left center of the envelope to give a well-balanced appearance.

A line beginning with "Attention of," or "Personal," should be typed at the lower left-hand side.

If a letter is being sent by Air Mail and/or Special Delivery, these words should be typed at the upper right-hand side, immediately under the postage stamp or stamps.

III. THE LANGUAGE
OF THE BUSINESS LETTER

The three basic tools for writing business letters are punctuation, spelling and grammar. For this reason we devote this chapter to the more important rules of punctuation and capitalization, as well as to the more common errors in English, and how to avoid them.

PUNCTUATION

It is impossible to put too much emphasis on the importance of correct punctuation. Its purpose is to break your sentences up into easily digested parts, and to make your meaning clear. It plays the same role in writing that breathing, pauses, and emphasis do in speaking.

Incorrect punctuation can change the entire meaning of a sentence. Leaving out periods, commas or other punctuation marks, or putting them in in the wrong places can result in your writing something contrary to what you intended to say.

The Period (.)

The period should be used at the end of every statement. It should be used at the end of every request. "We have your letter." "Please send 5 gross of pins." There are only three punctuation marks with which to end sentences: the period, the question mark, and the exclamation point.

The period should also be used to indicate that you have used an abbreviation, as in "Mr." which stands for "Mister"; "Dr." for "Doctor"; "Oct." for "October"; etc.

The Comma (,)

The comma indicates a short break in a sentence, and is used to make the meaning clear and the reading easy. A long sentence can be unintelligible without the proper use of commas. Notice the difference between the following sentences:

The goods you sent us which we ordered last May would have been fine items to sell our customers the cannery workers if they had not come after the peak season ending in June.

It would take several readings to make out the meaning of this sentence, but when properly punctuated, it is easily understood:

The goods you sent us, which we ordered last May, would have been fine items to sell our customers, the cannery workers, if they had not come after the peak season, ending in June.

In general, the comma should be used in the same way that you would use a pause in speaking. The basic rules for the use of the comma are:

(1) The comma is used to set off clauses, phrases and words that have a parenthetic function but for which parentheses are not suitable, as the following: that is, in fact, of course, it so happens that, etc.

(2) To set off words in apposition.

> Mr. Jones, our salesman, will call on you.

(3) To indicate a brief, direct quotation.

> Mr. Green said, "Please call on us."
> "Not this week," said your representative.

(4) To show that a word is missing.

> To err is human; to forgive, divine.

(5) To separate co-ordinate clauses which are joined by one of the conjunctions: and, but, for, either, or, neither, nor.

> The goods are not in stock, but shipment will be made when we get them.

(6) To separate lists of words.

> We ran short of cigarettes, candy, soda, pie, etc.

(7) To divide a sentence where identical or similar verbs follow one another.

> If you do it, do it now.

(8) To set off the name of the person you are addressing.

> Mr. James, please send us the coffee data.

(9) To divide series of figures into hundreds, thousands, ten thousands, etc.

> 7,585   57,585   8,564,784   585,758,494

(10) After the complimentary close of a letter.

> Yours truly,
> John Arnold

(11) To separate the parts of an address.

> Mother's Home Baked Pie Corp.,
> 239 Fall River Road,
> Hampton, Virginia.

(12) To separate the parts of the heading of a letter, the day of the month and the year.

> 639 Little Jones Street,
> New York, N. Y.,
> Sept. 3, 19——.

The Semicolon (;)

A semicolon indicates a shorter pause than a period, but a longer pause than a comma. It is used when a long sentence could well be broken into shorter ones but holds the thought together better when the break is not so sharp. It also serves to separate a series of clauses in a sentence:

This is what we can do for you: we can send part of your order now, that is, the Beethoven and Brahms records; we can send the whole order later on; we can cancel the order and let you take a chance on filling it elsewhere immediately.

The Colon (:)

The colon is used:

As an introduction to something that follows.

In salutations to letters, as, "Dear Sir:" (No dash or hyphen is required after the colon. "Dear Sir:—" is wrong.)

After expressions such as: for example: to wit: for instance: the following:

The Question Mark (?)

The question mark should be used after a direct question.

When can we expect shipment?

An indirect question does *not* need a question mark.

We want to know when we can expect shipment.

When two or more questions follow each other, a question mark should be used after each.

> Will you call on us? or shall we call on you?

The Exclamation Point (!)

The exclamation point indicates an emphatic statement that denotes surprise, emotion or doubt.

> The customer paid cash!
> We just can not put up with it!
> He says he shipped it!

The exclamation point is also used after exclamations, seldom used in business, such as: oh! ah! alas! ouch!

Unless it is used like seasoning in a soup, only a pinch now and then, the exclamation point defeats its own purpose. Most sentences carry more emphasis without an exclamation point than with them. Too many writers use exclamation points to lend excitement to sentences that are really not exciting at all.

Under no circumstances, should two or more exclamation points be used, one after the other.

The Dash (—)

The dash is used in a sentence where the thought is suddenly interrupted. It often serves the purpose of a colon, semicolon and comma alike, though these are more wisely used when the writer has learned their exact function.

Every time we ask you for payment—and that has had to be very often—you put us off with an excuse.

(No comma is required before the dash, as "often, —you." Use the dash alone, as "often—you.")

The Hyphen (-)

The hyphen is used to connect words and to divide them. It is also used when a word has to be divided between syllables at the end of a typewritten or printed line.

> Top-notch
> Anglo-American
> Air-conditioned
> Editor-in-chief
> Unfortunately, we are un-
> able to deliver your order.
> It is useless to wait indefi-
> nitely for his reply.

Be sure to divide such words by syllables, just as they are divided in the dictionary.

Parentheses ( )

Parenthesis marks make a slightly stronger break in a sentence than commas or dashes. They are most often used to enclose statements or references which amplify or explain the thought of the sentence. For example:

The fine brushes you sent us (and when I say "fine," I really mean it) are selling like hot cakes.

Parentheses are also used to enclose the figures of an amount that has been spelled out, such as: two hundred dollars ($200), etc.

Figures may be put in parentheses when a list is numbered consecutively: (1), (2), (3).

The Apostrophe (')

The apostrophe is used in forming possessives, and to indicate the omission of one or more letters in a word.

In most cases, the adding of the apostrophe and *s* forms the possessive, as in: John's hat, the company's headquarters, the month's billing.

In plural nouns, the apostrophe usually comes after the *s*, as in: the companies' headquarters, the months' billings.

Where the plural is not formed by *s*, the apostrophe is used in the same way it is in singular nouns, as for example: women's clothing, men's hats, children's habits.

When words that are singular end in *s*, the apostrophe is placed after the *s*, as in: Mathematics' laws are irrefutable.

Examples of words from which one or more letters have been omitted are:

> Can't—for cannot
> Don't—for do not
> I'm—for I am
> He's—for he is

Quotation Marks (" ")

Quotation marks are used to enclose all quotations which represent the exact words used.

The client said: "Sold!"

When another quotation is used within a quotation, single quotation marks are used.

He said: "When you answered, 'yes,' I wired the home office right away."

When the quotation takes up several paragraphs, quotation marks are placed at the beginning of each paragraph, but only at the end of the last paragraph.

CAPITALIZATION

Capitals should be used as follows:

(1) To begin the first word of every sentence, and every line of poetry.

(2) For proper names in general, names of people,

business firms, organizations, government committees, government boards, political parties, names of holidays, cities and states, months of the year, and days of the week.

(3) For the names of certain sections of the country: North, South, East and West; and their compounds: Northwest, Southeast, etc., except when they indicate merely a direction.

(4) For the titles of individuals when these accompany the name.

(5) For the first word of a quoted sentence, as in:

He said, "They will come."

SPELLING

If you don't know how to spell a word, look it up in the dictionary. Most accurate spellers avoid mistakes because they have learned to spell each word individually rather than because they have mastered a set of spelling rules.

The most frequent spelling mistakes are those to be found in the *ie* and *ei* words. A good way to keep the spelling of these words straight is to memorize LICENSE. You will find that the letter *i* almost always follows *l*, and the letter *e* almost always follows *c*.

Common exceptions to this rule are: height, foreign, siege, seize, neighbor, financier, weird, leisure, neither, sieve, reprieve.

ie	ei
believe	ceiling
liege	conceive
lien	deceive
relief	perceive
relieve	receive

SYLLABICATION

Syllabication is the separation of words into syllables. This is not only a guide to pronunciation, but a guide to the correct division of a word when there isn't room at the end of a line to write the entire word.

If you are at all doubtful about dividing a word into syllables, be sure to look it up in your dictionary. You will find, for example, that the word finger is written *fin'ger*. Should you have to split this word at the end of a line, you would write *fin-* at the end of the line and *ger* at the beginning of the next.

You must never divide words of one syllable, such as: width, waived, passed, mailed, filed, bounced, etc.

WRITING HINTS

It is true that the mechanics of the business letter, and the rules of punctuation, spelling and the like, are far simpler than the actual job of writing. But many people stare for minutes at a blank piece of paper, wondering how to begin, just because they have allowed themselves to build up a set of mental hazards. As a matter of fact, a little practice should convince anyone that it is as easy to write as it is to talk. If you can make a request or place an order orally, you can quickly learn to do so on paper.

The first thing to do in writing a business letter is to make sure of your facts. Then decide on the order of importance of the things you wish to say, and your letter is half written. It is really as easy as that.

Let us suppose that you wish to order a shipment of shoes. When you have before you the name and address of the concern to which you are writing, when you know the sizes, quantity, price and desired date of shipment of the shoes, you can hardly fail to write a good business letter.

Your letter, for instance, might read something like this:

Dear Sir:

   Please ship the following not later than May 3:

   2 gross Women's Oxfords, size 7-B, at $2.30 a pair.

   Our check for $662.40 in payment of this order is enclosed.

Yours truly,

This is a very simple form of business letter. But it is typical of all good business letters because it is brief and to the point.

Just as brevity is the soul of wit, so is brevity the soul of a business letter. Unlike the old-fashioned business letter which made use of many ornate, formal phrases, the modern business letter is as streamlined as a racing car. But under no circumstances should courtesy and clearness be sacrificed for brevity. The shortest business letter should always take time to be polite. And it must be as frank and open as a business conversation so that your correspondent will be convinced of your sincerity.

Many business letters do not have to go out of their way to be interesting. This is true of letters that place orders, answer inquiries, arrange for meetings and the like. But the letter which is written to persuade someone to do something is another story. This may be a sales letter; a letter asking for employment, for credit, and so on. In the letter asking for credit, it is important to interest the reader sufficiently to make him want to comply with your wishes. An example illustrating this type of letter follows:

Dear Sir:

As you know, we have done very well with the last shipment of fountain pens which you sent us. We sold the whole lot in a little less than two weeks. And we expect to do even better in the future.

You can help us to do this, if you will. We have outstanding a number of bills which we expect to be paid within a fortnight. Until then, we can order only the regular shipment of fountain pens on a cash basis. But if you are willing to extend our credit until the end of the month, we can place an order for double the amount with you.

Please let us know by Monday whether or not you can accommodate us.

Yours sincerely,

Notice that this letter talks about the correspondent's interests right from the start, and gives him an opportunity to make bigger sales. The language is simple and clear. In other letters, a richer style may be desirable. In all such letters there is one essential—a promise that the reader will get something from you, i.e., bigger sales, if he extends credit; a bargain, if he buys your product; a more effective organization, if he gives you the job for which you are applying.

"BUSINESS ENGLISH"

Many people think that there is a special language called "Business English" which is supposed to be somewhat different from everyday spoken English. Frequently this concept complicates the job of writing to a person with whom you are doing business. But the average business letter is written, not in some special "Business English," but in the familiar language which you use all day.

A business letter is usually shorter and clearer than a social letter. It may employ expressions used only in business, such as "order", "remit", "liabilities", "overhead". These expressions are used just as engineers, doctors and chemists use certain terms in their dealings with others.

There was a time when business letters were stiff and formal, but today the tendency is to write in a simple, natural, almost conversational way. Business correspondence ranges from letters that are almost as brief as telegrams, to more lengthy and intimate letters, depending on how well you know the person with whom you are dealing, and the requirements of the subject matter.

The best way to write a business letter is to make it conform as closely as possible to spoken English. Let us suppose that you have just received a letter from a wholesaler. He has promised you a shipment of goods which is late in arriving. You might telephone him and say:

"Mr. Jones, of the Jones-Hammond Company? How are you? This is Bill Rogers, of Rogers and Pratt. We've just received your letter about the shipment of brass couplings, but there seems to be some delay. I'm afraid our work is being held up until we get them. Will you please look into this and see that we get the couplings as soon as possible? Thank you. I know you'll do your best for us. Good-by."

If you decided to write to Mr. Jones instead of telephoning him, your letter might read:

Dear Mr. Jones:

Thank you for your letter of March 12, in which you promised immediate shipment of the brass couplings we ordered on March 6.

This shipment is several days overdue, and our work is being held up.

Will you please look into this and see what you can do about getting these couplings to us as soon as possible.

We know that you will do your best.

Yours cordially,

As you see, this typical business letter closely follows the telephone call. It is clear, brief and polite.

Avoiding "Dead" Expressions

Business letters used to be studded with stiff phrases that made up a sort of "Business English." Their function seemed to be to give business a sort of dignity. But now that business has come into its own, these expressions are only sand in the wheels of progress. We can be perfectly courteous without them, and we can be a great deal clearer and simpler, too.

Don't say: We beg to acknowledge your esteemed favor of September 16.
Say: We have your letter of September 16.

Don't say: Your letter at hand.
Say: We have your letter.

Don't say: We shall advise you.
Say: We shall let you know.

Don't say: As per your letter.
Say: According to your letter.

Don't say: And oblige.
Say: Thank you; or, thank you very much.

Don't say: We have your order and will forward same.
(Your correspondent knows that you have his order;
otherwise you wouldn't be writing about it.)
Say: We will forward your order at once.

Don't say: Thank you for yours of the 10th inst.
Say: Thank you for your letter of May 10.

Other expressions to be avoided are:

Don't say	*Say*
Enclosed please find	We enclose
We take pleasure	We are glad
Hand you a check	Send you a check
Owing to the fact that	Because
As to your proposition	Regarding your proposition
At an early date	Soon
At the present writing	Now
Even date	Today
In re the matter of	Regarding

IV. ROUTINE BUSINESS LETTERS

It should be the aim of every business office to answer all its mail the same day it is received. If for any good reason this is not possible, acknowledgment of the receipt of all letters should at least be made on the following day.

That all letters should be clear and courteous, goes without saying.

Here are example letters, sentences and phrases that may be used as a guide for the writing of the various types of business letters regarded as "routine" in most offices.

Acknowledgments

Mr. Howard Manchester
37 Jones Street
Little Falls, Nebraska

Dear Mr. Manchester:
We have your letter of June 10, and we are very pleased to hear from you.

You may rest assured that we will take up the matter you discussed with our Board of Directors as soon as possible. We shall be able to give you an answer within a week.

Yours sincerely,

Mrs. John H. Hoyt
27 Jane Street
Denver, Colorado

Dear Madam:

We were pleased to receive your inquiry of June 3. We carry a full line of straw hats, as the enclosed catalogue shows. Our price list is attached.

Your order will be greatly appreciated.

Very truly yours,

Mr. James Pearson
110 High Street
Minneapolis, Minn.

Dear Mr. Pearson:

Thank you for your letter of December 3. Because we have done business with each other for so long, I am going to make you a rather unusual proposition.

Present available prices are perfectly reasonable, but if you are buying for your spring trade we think you will do better to wait until the first of the year. If anything changes in the meantime I shall be very glad to let you know.

Cordially yours,

Beaver, Beaver & Pelt
211 MacDougal Street
Boston, Mass.

Gentlemen:

Thank you for your request for samples and quotations on one million Majestic Metal Clips.

Please allow us a few days to figure a price that would be fair for both of us. You may expect to hear from us within a week.

Very truly yours,

Mr. Harold Jasper
1900 Avenue C
New York City

Dear Mr. Jasper:

Ordinarily we would give you an immediate answer to your inquiry. However, the situation to date is that a change of policy is being contemplated. We shall be in a position to advise you by July 7th.

Yours sincerely,

Bates and Brown
Denver, Ohio

Dear Sirs:

We note that you have sent us your check for $15,000.17, whereas your total indebtedness comes to $18,000.03. We have made a thorough check of our books and think that the error is yours.

Please look into this as soon as you can, and if you agree

you owe us the remainder, please send it to us sometime this week because we are eager to close your account.

Yours truly,

Acme Manufacturing Co.
Barretsville, Mich.

Gentlemen:

Thank you for your letter of July 12. We have just placed an order for our summer sportswear, but we'd certainly like to keep you in mind for the Florida season.

Why don't you have your salesman drop in to see us as soon as he visits this territory?

Very truly yours,

Mr. W. W. Dawson, Pres.
Dawson-Jones Corp.
347 Fifth Street,
Boone, Conn.

Dear Mr. Dawson:

Thank you for your order of December 2.

We are prepared to ship immediately 87 pairs of white suede gloves, if you think that you can use the B Models instead of the C. Since most of our customers have found these satisfactory, we feel that you will too.

There is only a very slight difference in quality, but the low price makes these a very popular number.

Please let us know by phone or telegram by tomorrow evening.

Sincerely yours,

Opening Sentences and Phrases

This is to acknowledge your letter of April 1. We are immediately shipping 4 gross of mustard mills—812-B—F.O.B. Manchester Vermont. You should receive them within 2 or 3 days.

This is to confirm your wire dated May 14. We agree wholeheartedly with everything you say and will sign the contract as soon as you come into our office.

Regarding your telegram of July 7, we find it impossible to accept the conditions you set down.

Thank you for your letter dated August 12.

We were pleased to receive your letter of September 3.

The letter you mentioned in our telephone conversation has just reached us.

Thank you for such a quick confirmation of our telephone agreement.

The letter you referred to in last night's conversation has not yet reached us.

In reply to your letter of May 6, we are sorry to say that——.

We are sorry but the fur you speak about in your letter of July 8 cannot be repaired.

It is with great regret that we have to inform you that we cannot fill your order of November 11.

You will be glad to know that the request you made in your letter of July 27 has already been passed on to our Vice-President.

In answer to your letter of May 3.

Your letter of May 17 asks us to send you three bales.

Referring further to your inquiry of September 11.

Thank you for your letter, dated December 14. I will communicate with our field manager immediately.

Your telegram has just arrived. The order will be shipped tomorrow morning.

Thank you for your check.

We were pleased to receive your check in this morning's mail.

We are glad to learn from your letter of December 17, that——.

Ending Sentences and Phrases

We hope to hear from you soon.

Will you please tell us without delay what are your wishes in this matter?

Please tell us what decision you make—by return mail.

We are holding the goods while awaiting your reply.

We are always pleased to be of service to you in any way.

Please ask us for any further prices and samples you wish to have.

Please call on us when you need any further typewriter repairs.

STOPGAP LETTERS

Sometimes letters cannot be answered right away. In that case they should be acknowledged promptly and an explanation given for the delay. This often happens when information has been asked for and cannot be immediately answered or when the person to whom the letter is addressed is away from the office.

This is to acknowledge the samples which you sent to Mr. Foreman. Unfortunately, he has been called away from the office for a week. He will get in touch with you the moment he gets back.

Thank you for your inquiry of May 12. Unfortunately, we do not have all the information at our fingertips. A good deal will have to come from our branch office in Hartford. As soon as we get it, we will send all the details to you. Please be patient for a few days until we are able to write you again.

Thank you for your order of July 7. We are not yet sure whether or not we will be able to send you as many as two dozen gas generating machines. We could send you one dozen now and hold up your order for the others. Please let us know what you want to do in this matter.

The subject you are interested in will be brought up at the next meeting of the board of directors.

We are investigating the matter and will report to you as soon as we have the information.

CONFIRMING LETTERS

Mr. Hugo Bromfield
712 Elm Street
Bay Ridge, New Jersey

Dear Mr. Bromfield:

This is in reference to the call which your Mr. James made at our office this morning.

We hereby confirm the arrangements made between us respecting your terms and discount. In order to keep the record straight, here are the full terms of the agreement:

(Text of Agreement)

If this is all right please confirm; otherwise point out any inaccuracies so that it can be corrected right away.

Very truly yours,

It was nice to have a phone talk with you this morning. We are sending you samples immediately and will give you the price of 14¢ a pair.

Thank you for your call today. I look forward with pleasure to seeing you tomorrow (Tuesday) at 10:30.

Yes, indeed, I will be delighted to see you at 11:00 tomorrow morning. Please bring a contract with you. It will be a pleasure to sign it.

This is to confirm our telephone conversation today. Our Mr. Abernathy will be delighted to see you at 10:30 tomorrow morning. Please bring samples of your work with you.

Confirming the agreement we came to last Thursday, we shall undertake to——.

With further reference to the matter we discussed yesterday——.

MAKING INQUIRIES

You should be just as courteous in making an inquiry by mail as you would if you were making it in person. Just to say, bluntly, "Send us the following information," or "Send catalogue," may make your correspondent think that you are not a very pleasant person to deal with. Here are a number of letters typical of a kind which business men use to smooth the path of their business relationships.

Mr. William R. Brown
Wilton, N. Y.

Dear Bill:
This may be a trade secret. But what are a few secrets between old friends? I am very eager to know who designed the packages you are using for your prunes. That is one of the most striking packages I have seen this season, and I would certainly like to get my hands on your de-

signer. Since we are not competitors (at least in business), I am sure you will be glad to send us this information with the speed of light.

Sincerely,

Jones-Smith Corporation
Potter Blvd.
Brooklyn, N. Y.

Dear Sirs:

We are in the market for heavy rubber shower curtains printed with a flower pattern with matching window drapes.

What price could you quote us on three dozen pairs?

Please let us know by phone or telegraph within 48 hours.

Yours sincerely,

Abernathy and Smith
31 Rover Road
San Francisco, Cal.

Gentlemen:

We would appreciate it if you would let us know whether or not rayon sportswear shirts and twill, gabardine, sharkskin, and stripes come in size $16\frac{1}{2}$.

It will be to your interest to give us this information as quickly as possible.

Yours truly,

Joe Jones Hat Stores
Chrysler Building
New York, N. Y.

Gentlemen:

We are making a survey of the buying habits of American customers.

Could you let us know whether you have sold more brown hats or gray in the last year?

We will greatly appreciate an answer to this inquiry.

Sincerely yours,

Jones-O'Brien, Inc.
816 Little Bear St.
Chicago, Ill.

Gentlemen:

Can you please quote us a price on 50 gross of your 71 × 84 reversible wool blankets, 15% reused wool and 85% cotton, bound with rayon satin, colors mahogany and cedar.

Very truly yours,

McGonigle & Johnson, Inc.
97 Duane Street
New York, N. Y.

Gentlemen:

Please let us know if your model 7B, 6 × 4 wash cloths come in pale blue. We would like to have this information promptly because we expect to place an order within a few weeks.

Yours truly,

Athens Box Co.
East Rock Road
Washington, D. C.

Gentlemen:

Would you be so kind as to send us a complete statement of the goods we have bought from you this year.

We wish to check our books before we get your final monthly statement.

Yours sincerely,

Manhattan Supply Co.
Laurel Street
Long Island City, N. Y.

Dear Sirs:

We have been pleased with your tabulating machine and wish to order two new ones this fall.

However, we would like to know if it is true that you are making a faster machine than your model V, which we have been using up to date.

Yours very truly,

Sentences and Phrases

How soon can you deliver 500 folders of the same size and quality as the samples we enclose?

Please tell us if there is any special way in which you would like us to package the goods you ordered.

Would you be kind enough to send us the following information as soon as possible?

May we ask for the following data, if it is not against your policy to give out such information?

Will you please tell us

Will you kindly inform me whether

Would you be so kind as to inform me

May I ask you to inform me

I should greatly appreciate your telling me

May I request the following information?

Do you happen to know whether or not

I should be glad to know whether

I shall greatly appreciate it if you will

Are you in a position to know

Is it possible for you to obtain the following information for me?

ANSWERING INQUIRIES

The letter you write to answer inquiries should be just as courteous as the answer you would make in person. When you give information, you should appear glad to give it. If, for any reason whatever, you are unable to give your correspondent the information that he wants you should be genuinely sorry not to be able to do so. The following are typical of the answers people like to receive.

North American Marketing Institute
15 Wisconsin Blvd.
Chicago, Ill.

Gentlemen:

Thank you for your interest in our firm.

In answer to your inquiry of September 12, we are sorry to say that we cannot divulge any of our sales secrets. We hope that this will not inconvenience you too greatly.

Sincerely yours,

Wool Furnishing Corp.
St. James Road
St. Paul, Minn.

Dear Sirs:

We are pleased to receive your inquiry for a price on 50 gross reversible wool blankets, 71 × 84, 15% reused wool and 85% cotton bound with rayon satin, colors mahogany and cedar.

We can give you a price of $20,000, F.O.B., Chicago.

Shall we hold these goods for your order?

Sincerely yours,

Mr. Leslie Roberts, Buyer
Sportswear Shirts & Pants Co.
Santa Monica, Cal.

Dear Sir:

In reply to your inquiry, we are sorry to say that our rayon sports shirts and twill, gabardine, sharkskin and stripes do not come in any size larger than size 16.

We will send you our new spring catalogue as soon as it comes off the press, in the event that any of our other sports shirts would be of interest to you.

Sincerely yours,

Household Furniture Co.
906 Driscoll Ave.
New York, N. Y.

Dear Sirs:

We are glad to send you the information you requested.
Our Model 7B, 6 × 4 wash cloth does come in pale blue. We are enclosing a sample.

Sincerely yours,

Mr. Joseph Sellers
396 Madison Ave.
New York, N. Y.

Dear Joe:

The fellow who designed my prune packages is an old friend of mine, by the name of Howard Johnson. He lives at 24 Jones Street, New York City, and his phone number is Perry 3–1931.

Sincerely yours,

Mr. Walter Sutton
Sutton & Pratt Wholesalers
24 Teaneck St.
Paterson, New Jersey

Dear Mr. Sutton:

This is in confirmation of the telegram we sent you December 28.

Our price for three dozen pairs of heavy rubber shower curtains printed with a flower pattern and matching drapes would be $80.00.

Shall we hold them for your order?

Sincerely yours,

Mr. Jasper Means, Office Manager
Lead Pencil Co.
81 Pearl St.
Yonkers, New York

Dear Mr. Means:

In response to your inquiry about chartering three buses for your office outing, we are glad to say that we can make arrangements with you.

Our local manager would like to see you tomorrow morning at 10:30. Will you call him at Jerome 9–2100 to confirm the appointment?

Sincerely yours,

Williams Manufacturing Co.,
347 Cherry Street
Sylvania, N. Y.

Gentlemen:

With reference to your request of November 15, we herewith enclose a statement of your October account.

Frankly, you have put us in quite a spot. While we appreciate your wish to have a complete statement of the goods you bought from us this year, your request at this time presents certain difficulties.

However, if you will wait a few days, we will be able to send the information to you.

Yours very truly,

Robert Schofield Company
27 Allen Street
Seattle, Washington

Gentlemen:

Thank you for your inquiry as to the earliest date on which we can ship you 500 folders of the same size and quality as the samples you enclosed. We can make shipment any time after Thursday. We are awaiting instructions from you.

Very truly yours,

Sentences and Phrases

We are glad to answer your inquiry. The only packaging requirement we have is that every item be wrapped in cotton to protect it against breakage.

We are glad to send you the information you desire.

Since it is not against our policy to give you the information you request we are pleased to send you the full details.

As requested in your letter, we send

As desired by you

At the request of your sales manager, we are pleased to

We are glad to forward as desired

Here is the information you request

We are sorry that we are unable to ascertain

Unfortunately we cannot tell

We have no way of getting the information you desire

SECRETARIAL LETTERS

Here are letters that a secretary writes in her employer's absence, or when her employer is too busy to write them himself. While any of the letters in this book could, with slight changes, be signed by a secretary, there are specific sorts of letters that a secretary is more likely to sign. These, for the main part, are letters of acknowledgment and also stopgap letters.

Dear Mr. Jones:

Mr. John Rogers asks me to convey his regrets in not being able to answer your letter until the end of next week. Just now he is engaged in a complete reorganization of our Detroit office.

Mr. Rogers wants to assure you that he will answer your inquiry in complete detail as soon as he has finished this job.

Sincerely yours,
N. K. Slocum,
Secretary to Mr. Rogers

Dear Mr. Smythe:

Mr. John J. Hammond asks me to write you that he cannot see you next Wednesday at 3:00. However, he will be able to give you all the time you need next Friday at 4:00.

Very truly yours,
Katherine Rogers
Secretary to Mr. Hammond

Dear Mr. James:

As Mr. Fletcher will be in Des Moines until the first of the month, I am writing to acknowledge your inquiry of May 3. I am sure that Mr. Fletcher will answer you in detail as soon as he gets back.

Sincerely yours,
Jane O'Reilly
Secretary to Mr. Fletcher

V. LETTERS ABOUT GOODS
AND SERVICES

The only way to get exactly what you want is to be as specific as possible. This holds true whether you are actually ordering goods, or just inquiring about goods, offers, samples or prices. You should cover all of these questions: What? How many? For how much? Where? When? How? This is your one and only insurance of getting just what you want, at the time for which you have ordered it, delivered to the right place, and at the indicated price and terms.

You should give complete information about the following points:

Description
    Article
    Catalogue number
    Size
    Color
    Model
    Other specifications
Quantity

Unit Price

Discount (if for resale or if bills are discounted for prompt
payment)

Total price

Place to which goods are to be shipped

Means of shipment

Terms

Purchase order number

Date of order

Signature of person authorized to order

You cannot be too specific in the directions you
give. For example, it is not always enough to mention
a color such as blue if you are ordering clothing; you
want an exact shade of blue, and you should state it.
In just such a way should you break your order down
into the most minute details covering every aspect
of it. It is always dangerous to assume that your correspondent will take something for granted. You will
never have any disappointments if everything you
want is down in black and white.

If you have occasion to make a great number of
purchases you will find it convenient to use a printed
order form. This saves time since it prevents unnecessary typing and covers all the requirements, which
merely have to be filled in or checked.

There is one motto which should continually stay
in the mind of a person who writes any business letter
whatsoever, and especially one who places an order.
It is this: *Always keep carbons.*

One prominent business man says that he keeps carbons even when he leaves a note for the milkman. This may be an exaggerated precaution, but there are many sad stories of businesses which have been thrown into considerable disorder because somebody neglected to make a carbon copy and to keep it conveniently filed.

Always make out your orders in duplicate at least. Do this whether you use a printed order form or not. If your organization is large enough to have a receiving department, make out the order in triplicate. And if there is a special auditing department, make out a special carbon for it.

There is only one exception to the rule of giving detailed descriptions of the article you order; that is, when you are ordering from a house that makes a single product. Obviously, if you are ordering packages of breakfast food from a one-brand cereal manufacturing company, it is enough to state that you want one-pound packages of that breakfast food, without describing the color of the box. However, when you are ordering from a house that manufactures or distributes a number of articles, you must for your own protection specify the one you want.

Let us say that you are ordering silk stockings. Your requirements might be the following: catalogue number 35; size 9½; light beige color; 50% pure silk, 50% weighted silk; full-fashioned extra long; 3 gauge silk crepe; reinforced heels and toes;

lisle top. Omit any one of these details, and you are likely to receive merchandise other than that which you had in mind.

Don't forget to include the catalogue number of the article when you are ordering from a catalogue, and just for an added precaution, mention the date or number of the catalogue.

Sometimes it is advisable to make shipping instructions general. You might ask to have goods shipped "the cheapest way" or "as quickly as possible." Usually it is advisable to be as definite as possible about shipping instructions. You specify "Via Parcel Post," "Via Express," "Via Air Express," "Via Fast Freight, Pennsylvania Railroad," "Via National Carloading Company," "Via Mercury Bus," etc.

Terms of the order may relate to the shipment when, for example, you order the goods "C.O.D.," or "F.O.B. San Francisco." They may refer to payment when, for instance, you specify: "2% ten days or 60 days net." They may cover the date of delivery when you write something like: "If you can make delivery by August 10, please send us the following, etc."

It is very important for an order to include both the purchase order number and the date for purposes of identification.

The date should be complete, showing the month, the day of the month, and the year. The date, however, is not sufficient by itself, since frequently one or more orders will be sent to the same house on the same day.

With the purchase order number on the label of the package the recipient can readily identify the merchandise and arrange for its disposal.

An order is invalid unless it is signed by someone who is authorized to do so. This authority is usually vested in members of a purchasing department who receive the authority from the heads of other departments. In small organizations, it is usually the owner of the business who places his signature upon the order.

ASKING FOR PRICES AND SAMPLES

Brothers Hotel Supply Co.
1195 North Ave.
New York, N. Y.

Gentlemen:

We enclose details of our inquiry for dishes to be delivered before the first of next month.

Will you please give us your prices for the quantity named?

Yours truly,

Chicago Clothiers, Inc.
Morton Ave. & South Blvd.
Chicago, Ill.

Gentlemen:

We require samples in your very lowest prices of navy and black serge. The quantity required is 10,000 yards of each and deliveries spread equally over the next eight months.

Please note that your quotation and samples must be delivered no later than the 8th of this month.

Yours truly,

The Chatham Pen Co.
Reedston, Oregon

Gentlemen:

Please send us samples and your lowest prices for your fountain pens, model 464-B. Samples and prices must reach us no later than the 15th of this month.

Yours very truly,

ORDERING GOODS

Gillette-Burns Co.
411 Gleenwood Street
Cleveland, Ohio

We enclose our check for $48.12. Please send the following items to be shipped by prepaid express. The order is contingent on our receiving the terms of 2%—30 days:

1 doz. linen handkerchiefs	.06	$ .72
1 pair Majestic Garters, silk finish	.50	.50
4 pair White Suede Gloves, size 6½	1.50	6.00
6 each White Oxford Sport Shirts	2.00	12.00
5 pair Black Lisle Socks	.40	2.00
	TOTAL	21.22

Sincerely yours,

Rogers Chemical Supply Co.
10 E. 22 Street
Omaha, Neb.

Gentlemen:

Please ship the following goods by motor freight at the earliest possible moment and charge to our account:

15 lbs. bicarbonate of soda	@ .30	$ 4.50
1 gross boxes, yeast extract	@ .25	36.00
45 bottles Cod Liver Oil—#47 B @ $1.00		45.00
	TOTAL	$85.50

Very truly yours,

Dodge Supply Company
Lawrence, Ill.

Gentlemen:

This is to confirm my telephone order of yesterday for the following items:

    4 Jr. Sewing Machines Model 3A
    7 Homemaker's Ironing Boards
   15 Fold Up Clothes Racks

Yours sincerely,

Johnstone Company
Main Street
Verona, Mo.

Gentlemen:

We enclose confirmation for our order given your salesman on January 12.

Yours very truly,

Men's Wearing Apparel
Linden Avenue
Maspeth, Mass.

Gentlemen:

Thank you for your samples of striped coatings received today. Please make shipment in accordance with our Order No. 2602 enclosed herewith.

> Yours truly,

Barnes & Barnes
Fruit Dealers
1930 Sheepshead Bay Rd.
Sheepshead Bay, N. Y.

Gentlemen:

Enclosed is a trial order for delivery June 22.

Please send in one lot complete, packed in burlap, shipped by freight, New York, New Haven & Hartford, as per our order.

> Yours truly,

Modern Maid Fashions
25 East Tenth Street
Chicago, Ill.

Gentlemen:

Enclosed is an order to which we ask your special attention with regard to time of delivery. It is important that we receive these goods on the exact day mentioned as we have advertised largely the day of our sale.

Please let us know promptly if you have any difficulty

in supplying the exact goods ordered. All orders must be delivered complete; no remainders must follow.

Sincerely yours,

Sentences and Phrases

Please send us the following items C.O.D.

We are enclosing our check for $234.56. Please send us the following items.

Will you please send, and charge to our account, the following:

We are glad to send you our order No. 475. Please notice that it gives full instructions for billing and shipping.

Please bill us on the usual terms for the following:

ACKNOWLEDGING ORDERS

Orders should be acknowledged immediately. Remember that when you acknowledge an order you may be making a tacit acceptance of conditions to which you cannot agree. A carelessly worded acknowledgment can often lead to a lawsuit, that is, if you carelessly make commitments as to prices, date of shipment and other details when you are not able to fulfill them.

Johnson-Thompson Co.
Waterville, Colo.

Gentlemen:

This is to acknowledge your order for 15 lbs. of bicarbonate of soda, 45 bottles cod liver oil, 1 gross boxes yeast extract.

If we are to ship goods by date requested in your order we can send you only 40 bottles cod liver oil instead of 45 bottles. The other goods will be sent complete.

We shall be able to fill the rest of the order within a week. We hope that this will be satisfactory.

Yours very truly,

G. A. Barrett & Bros.
Hanover, Kentucky

Gentlemen:

We have received your order for which we thank you. Please let us know if you do not receive the goods within 4 days as we try to fill all orders within 24 hours of receipt.

Very truly yours,

The Stafford Co.
Wilmington, Del.

Gentlemen:

Thank you for your order ⌗411 for 6 dozen poster mountings. We would like to point out that the price agreed upon was $72.00 each, not $74.00 as stated in your order. We are holding the goods until we hear from you.

Very truly yours,

S. T. Goodman Corp.
Denver, Colorado

Dear Sirs:

Acknowledging your valued order of January 9, we regret that we cannot ship until January 23. Please let us know if this is satisfactory so that we can make shipment on that date.

Very truly yours,

Sentences and Phrases

Thank you for your order. It will receive our immediate attention.

This is to acknowledge your order. We try to fill all orders within 24 hours.

We have received your order, and will fill it at once.

SHIPMENTS AND DELIVERIES

Every letter giving notice of shipment should cover the following three points: Type of Merchandise, Date of Shipment, Method of Shipping. Notice of shipment enables the purchaser to check with the transportation company when the goods do not reach him promptly. Thus a tracer can be sent if the goods are overdue.

Newman & Newman
Opolis, Texas

Gentlemen:

We are very sorry to hear, according to your letter of January 28, that you have not received the 20 dozen overalls you ordered on January 18. We have checked with our shipping department and have found that the goods were shipped by Santa Fe freight on January 23.

We have sent a tracer to the railroad company and expect to have a telegram tomorrow morning. If we cannot locate your goods within the next few days, we will be very glad to duplicate the order.

We trust this will be satisfactory.

Yours sincerely,

C. P. Jennings, Inc.
Austin, Texas

Gentlemen:

We thank you for your order of July 7, which has just been received. It will be given our prompt attention. Should you find it necessary to write regarding this order, please mention our File No. 3189.

Very truly yours,

Sentences and Phrases

This letter notifies you that your order for 72 Bridge Tables, No. 188, dated July 7, was shipped today via Transcontinental Railroad.

We acknowledge with thanks the receipt of your Order No. 3127, dated July 10, for the following:

This letter acknowledges the receipt of your order of

This is to thank you for your order of November 10. It is being shipped today. Invoice and bill of lading are enclosed.

Many thanks for your order of yesterday which has been forwarded to our plant for immediate manufacture. Delivery will be made October 5.

Thank you for your letter advising us that you have shipped our order for 10 cartons Animal Food by Santa Fe freight.

FOLLOW-UPS

Last week, we wrote to you for some information about your Fall Catalogue. There is one more question we would like to ask.

Thank you for your letter of August 12. We would like the following additional information.

Have you received the samples which we shipped you May 4?

Before you decide where you are going to place the order you discussed with us, we wish you would look into the following matter.

This letter is to remind you that the samples we sent you represent only the most popular numbers in stock. If you wish to see others, we shall be glad to send them to you.

This is to supplement our letter of July 7. We neglected to mention that we can give you free delivery anywhere within the United States.

BARGAINING LETTERS

The arguments of bargaining are to suggest to the seller that you are not in great need of his products, that his product is not worth as much as he says it is, and that you would not find it difficult to obtain the same product somewhere else at a lower price. The seller's method is to persuade the buyer that the latter does need his product, that the product is worth the full price, and that the product is superior to all others of the same kind. In all cases the bargaining must be carried on with as much courtesy as possible.

Ronald Drug Company
421 Swan Boulevard
Detroit, Mich.

Dear Sirs:

We have been very pleased with your product, as you know. However, we find that we can obtain a price of $4.00 per hundred with a concern in our locality, which is 50 cents per hundred lower than your price.

If you can see your way clear to meeting these figures we would be pleased to place with you an order that will carry us for the rest of this year. That order is likely to be one of the largest that we have ever placed with you.

Yours truly,

Bryant & Cardinal
421 Maple Avenue
Minneapolis, Minn.

Gentlemen:

We are aware of the fact that your office equipment is about the best on the market. We realize that your materials are of the very highest quality and that you pay about the highest wages in the field.

Nevertheless, we would prefer handling lower quality goods if we could get a lower price. Our customers do not demand the standard of quality that you put into your equipment. If we are to continue to deal with you we must ask for a 7½% reduction in price in order that we may achieve a higher volume of sales. We shall wait for a price from you before we decide where to place our next order.

Yours truly,

Rogers & Pratt
21 Fairfax Avenue
Boston, Massachusetts

Dear Sirs:

We regret that it is not possible to accept the reduced price you offer. It was very kind of you to suggest meeting us half way, but this will not be enough to make allowances for our increased overhead and advertising. Since we do not agree with you that we cannot get the same quality of goods somewhere else, we feel perfectly justified in our firmness about the matter.

Unless you see your way clear to grant us an additional reduction in price, we are afraid that we will have to sever our very pleasant relationship with you.

Yours cordially,

Answering the Bargaining Letter

Smith & Jones Wholesale Company
95 Broadway
New York, New York

Dear Sirs:

Thank you for your letter of June 12. In view of the fact that we have done business with each other for so long and that you have bought from us such a volume of office equipment, we would like to meet you half way in your request for lower prices.

May we suggest an overall reduction of 4% in price, which will hold right down the line.

Since our own overhead has increased somewhat in the last few months, this offer on our part is good only for a few months. At the end of that time you will have to go back to the previous price list.

Our sales manager, Mr. Smith, will call on you with some display material which should help you to effect a higher volume of sales.

Yours sincerely,

Smith & Jones
West 24th Street
New York, N. Y.

Gentlemen:

After discussing the matter with our Board of Directors, we have decided to comply with your request for lower prices. Attached is a corrected price list for our merchandise.

Yours very truly,

Peabody & Smith
7 Duane Street
Macon, Georgia

Dear Sirs:

In reference to your letter of May 7, we cannot make a better offer than the one we suggested to you. We feel that that offer itself is really generous under the circumstances.

Checking our books, we find that you have purchased from us twice as much the first three months of this year as you did in the first three months of last year. This indicates to us that you have been successful in retailing our merchandise.

We hope that you will be able to accept our offer, upon reconsideration, because we have been very pleased to have you on our list of accounts.

Yours truly,

O'Brien Drugstore
492 Little Elm Street
Syracuse, New York

Dear Sirs:

We are sorry to say it is not possible for us to meet the price you requested in your letter of November 9.

If you care to place an order with us any time in the future, you may be assured of the same prompt attention which you have had in the past.

Yours very truly,

VI. LETTERS OF COMPLAINT
AND ADJUSTMENT

WRITING LETTERS OF COMPLAINT

The purpose of writing a letter of complaint is to get better service or to effect an adjustment, unless you are just writing to sever your relationships. The more specific your letter, the easier it will be for your correspondent to handle your complaint.

John Marshall Jones & Co.
94 Jefferson Street
New York, N. Y.

Gentlemen:

We have had a good deal of trouble because of the fact that your goods are sent to our receiving department frequently after 5:00 P.M. Furthermore, your deliveries have frequently arrived well after the time specified in our letter of May 12. Unless we get better co-operation from you in the future we shall have to abide by the strict terms of our contract and cancel all further orders.

Sincerely yours,

R. C. Weathers & Co.
51 Pilgrim Place
Boston, Mass.

Gentlemen:

We are sorry to say that your shipment of 10 Ironing Boards received today at the Hartford depot (New York, New Haven & Hartford R.R.) was so greatly damaged that we are unable to accept it.

May we remind you that according to the terms of our contract goods in perfect condition are to be received by us on or before next Thursday. Please send us your advice by telegram.

Yours truly,

The Green-Brown Co.
444 Elm Street
Scott, Pa.

Gentlemen:

We are obliged to return to you the shipment which we received today. This is order 47–8 dated March 17.

The china was so poorly packed that six of the cups were broken.

There are shortages as follows: 5 cups, 3 plates, and 7 saucers.

Please make good the damaged items, and forward the rest of the order so that we may have it for our weekend sale.

Very truly yours,

J. Walter Smith Recording Company
Bryant Avenue
San Francisco, Calif.

Gentlemen:

Twelve of the 150 records I ordered from you last Thursday were completely smashed when they arrived at the depot here.

I am enclosing a carbon copy of our order with asterisks after the name of each of the broken records. Please get them to us within twenty-four hours if possible, because our customer is very eager to have them.

Yours sincerely,

Oldtown Mfg. Co.
Oldtown, Ohio

Gentlemen:

We do not like to go over the head of your New York manager, but we find in this case that it is necessary to do so.

Your New York branch has made so many mistakes in filling our orders, has so consistently ignored our request for information, and has made so many mistakes in its billing, that we suspect the manager is not very interested in keeping our business.

Since we have had such pleasant dealings with you in the past, we wish to give you this opportunity to correct the situation. What can you do about it?

Sincerely yours,

Acme Machine Co.
Springfield, Wis.

Dear Sirs:

The stamping machine we bought from you on May 6 is "unconditionally guaranteed for a year." We find that the machine has broken down completely. We have had a mechanic in to look it over. He reports that the rotators appear to have been cracked before the machine was installed.

Since you have no service man in this territory we intend to return the machine to you collect, and expect to receive a new one within a few days.

Very truly yours,

Beats-all Pen Corp.
Bigville, N. J.

Dear Sirs:

A number of our customers have been complaining that your fountain pens leak badly. We have lost a good deal of time because of this and have been put to considerable expense for cleaning bills.

Curiously, we have had trouble only with your last shipment of fountain pens. The ones we received before that were more than one hundred per cent satisfactory.

Please check with your manufacturing department to see if there is any error in the making of these pens, and also to find out if they are packed with adequate protection for shipment.

We are returning the entire remainder of these pens,

two gross. We hope that the shipment you send us in return will not give us any trouble.

Yours sincerely,

Everybody's Emporium
Detroit, Mich.

Gentlemen:

Somebody in your organization has made a mistake, perhaps accidental, in filling the order I sent in last Wednesday.

I ordered a gray hat size 7½, Model 27B.

I received a green hat size 8, Model 31D.

I am returning the second hat, and would like, in substitution, to receive the first one as quickly as possible.

Yours sincerely,

Caslon Company,
Louisville, Ky.

Gentlemen:

Referring to your letter advising us of the shipment of our Order ⚹8219, we see that you have sent this by airmail express although we did not specify it. Since we were in no special hurry to receive these goods, we cannot accept the extra charge. We feel that we are justified in subtracting this from our bill.

Yours sincerely,

Smith Brothers,
947 Maple Avenue,
Newtown, Wash.

Attention: Credit Manager

Dear Sir:

Years of business dealings develop, of course, an understanding attitude about slip-ups, but we feel that in order to keep the records straight, we have to take exception to the letter received from you in the afternoon mail.

Exactly eight days after we sent you remittance in full for a month's account, we received what is apparently your last and toughest collection letter.

Possibly your clerk meant to send us a gentle reminder that our account was due, but instead he implied that we were in for a lawsuit. We're pretty sure you are not careless in general, so we are not going to say anything more about the matter, but please see that this doesn't happen again.

Very truly yours,

H. T. Brown & Co.
Milltown, Mo.

Dear Sirs:

Our agreement with you is that we are to be billed at 25% off the list price. There has apparently been a slip-up in the billing department. We are therefore returning your last bill for correction.

Sincerely yours,

ANSWERING COMPLAINTS

The customer is always entitled to an explanation, whether he has a real or imagined cause of complaint. If you wish to keep his business, it is important for you to answer his complaint as specifically and as promptly as possible.

Please note that while many of the following letters admit mistakes and apologize for them, none of the letters makes an abject apology. Since you wish always to make the best possible impression on your correspondent, it is very unwise to deprecate yourself or your organization. When you *are* in the wrong, admit it, pass it off, and offer a solution to the error as quickly as you can.

Plaza Music Store
Cornwall, Calif.

Dear Sirs:

Thank you for your courteous letter dated April 27

We were sorry to hear that 12 of the 150 records you ordered last Thursday arrived in a damaged condition.

We are immediately shipping replacements of those records.

We are also discontinuing the new method of packaging with which we have been experimenting, as we do not care to rely upon it when it has failed even once.

Yours sincerely,

Timberlake & Co.
Girard, Neb.

Gentlemen:

We certainly intend to live up to the strict terms of our guarantee. If you wish to return the stamping machine you bought from us on May 6, we will pay for the freightage and send you another one in its place.

Before you do this, we would like to make another suggestion. It is possible that the mechanic who looked at your machine is not thoroughly familiar with its construction. Furthermore, we have a service man in the territory adjacent to yours who will be glad to come in, inspect the machine, and arrange for any necessary repairs.

This would enable you to put your machine in use within a few days if the damage is minor, and we hope that this suggestion will be favorably received by you.

Our service man, Mr. J. M. Smith, has instructions to telephone you Thursday morning.

Yours truly,

Mr. Richard Millington,
339 Summit Street
Cloverdale, Mich.

Dear Mr. Millington:

With reference to your letter of November 5, we are very sorry that we sent you a green hat size 8, Model 31D, in place of the hat you ordered. Your gray hat size 7½, Model 27B is probably on its way to you now, since we ordered it shipped on receipt of your letter.

The mistake, as you surmised, was accidental. Your

order was filled by a clerk who has had only a few weeks' experience. We will take great care to see that this sort of error does not take place again.

Yours truly,

Hood-Stetson Corp.
Jacksonville, Fla.

Gentlemen:

We are investigating your claim as to Order 47–8 dated March 17.

While we have not been able to locate the reasons for the unsatisfactory packaging and the shortage, we are immediately sending replacements for the damaged goods and completing your order. It is possible that the cups were broken in transit, but we do not wish to hold up your weekend sale.

As soon as we have been able to trace the causes, we will let you know. You may rest assured that we will make every effort to give you satisfactory service in the future.

Sincerely yours,

Mr. Harold D. Noel, Pres.
The Noel-Richards Company
Garnett, N. J.

Dear Mr. Noel:

We cannot thank you enough for your letter of July 9. Up to the present, we have had no idea that our New York branch was not handling your account to your complete satisfaction.

For the time being, we are making it possible for your orders to be dealt with directly through this office. Meanwhile, we are sending a special field investigator to make a thorough analysis of the New York situation.

At present it is impossible for us to tell what changes we may have to make in our New York office. What we do know is that we intend to give you complete satisfaction, whether any changes become necessary or not.

Yours truly,

Pelton Brothers
83 Tenth Street
Boston, Mass.

Gentlemen:

When we shipped your Order 8219 by airmail express instead of by parcel post we were assuming that you needed prompt delivery of the merchandise. Although this inaccurate guess was made in your interest, we are very happy to accept the extra charge.

Yours sincerely,

The Corner Store
Main and Madison Streets
Middletown, Md.

Dear Sirs:

Thank you for returning our last shipment of fountain pens. All we hope is that you returned them at our expense. We have just found a flaw in our manufacturing process due to the installation of a time-saving machine which we have recently put in.

You may be certain that our pens will be as satisfactory to you in the future as they have been in the past. We are shipping you replacements immediately. We are taking the liberty of sending you an extra dozen, at no cost, as a small compensation for your trouble.

Yours sincerely,

J. B. Nosuch & Co.
Parkwood, Oregon

Gentlemen:

We certainly do owe you an apology.

The clerk who sent you the collection letter instead of reminding you that your account was due has just been transferred to another department where we hope she will not be so dangerous.

As always, you are good for all the credit you want.

Yours sincerely,

John Jones & Son
Belmont, Mo.

Dear Sirs:

Thank you for returning our last bill for correction. We will certainly see to it that you get the usual 25% off the list price. We are very sorry for the slip-up in our billing department.

Yours very truly,

Mrs. Lincoln Jones
Blank, Vermont

Dear Madam:

We were rather astonished to receive your letter of April 4. We are perfectly willing to admit that we are partly to blame in the matter. But we would hate to think that our whole organization is what you say it is.

Of course, we are sending you a new dressing gown immediately. If you are as fair as we have reason to believe you are, we think you might wish to drop in and have a talk with us before you take your account to some other store. We know that we have served you satisfactorily in the past, and we are sure that we can do so in the future.

Yours sincerely,

VII. LETTERS ABOUT CREDIT

To Customers Asking for Credit Information

The first thing you ought to know about a person who asks for credit is: *"Can* he pay?" The next most important question is: *"Will* he pay?"

It is never a sound idea to take the answer to either of these questions for granted. Some firms can pay but don't; some firms want to pay but can't.

Luckily, asking for credit references is such a formality that almost all companies will take your inquiry for a formality rather than for an expression of doubt. Even if you do have any doubts in your mind, it might be ruinous to your business dealings to allow them to creep into your letter.

Here are some courteous matter-of-fact examples of letters that ask for credit information.

Smith and Jones,
Browntown, Minn.

Gentlemen:
We are in receipt of your order of yesterday which has had our careful attention.

With reference to this order, we fail to find your name on our books, and we are therefore enclosing a credit application blank which we should be glad to have you fill out and return to us so that we may make shipment at the earliest possible moment.

We hope that this transaction may lead to a mutually profitable business connection between us.

Sincerely yours,

William Green Co.
Whiteville, N. M.

Dear Sirs:

Thank you for your order of the twenty-third, in which we note you ask that the goods be charged.

We are glad to have your name on our books, and we have opened a credit account for you. So that we may complete our records, will you please give us the name of some firm with whom you already have a credit account, or the names of any of our customers who recommended us to you. As you know, this is the usual procedure in opening a credit account for a new firm.

Yours very truly,

Mrs. Cleveland Jones
Green Groves, N. J.

Dear Mrs. Jones:

Thank you for your request to be placed on our books as a charge customer.

Your standing is such that we have placed you on our

books immediately. However, our custom is to have two or more credit references in our files. If you don't mind will you please send us the names of two or more stores with which you have charge accounts, along with the name of the bank in which you have a checking account.

Please feel free to order whatever you like, in the meantime.

Sincerely yours,

Bill's Stationery Store,
Jeffersonville, Utah.

Gentlemen:

Thank you for the order which we received yesterday.

Since we do not have the privilege of your name on our books, we should very much appreciate your sending us a check for the amount, or the names of two trade references in case you want to open a monthly account with us.

Yours very truly,

Evans and Roberts
Moberly, New Hampshire

Gentlemen:

It is a pleasure to receive your order of September 12 for women's shoes. We hope that this is the first of many orders which you may place with us.

We notice that your letter does not mention any method of payment.

You are no doubt aware of the custom of the wholesale

trade that opening orders are payable in cash. If you wish us to send the shoes immediately we shall be glad to do so on receipt of your remittance for $90.00.

Pending an answer from you, we have packed the shoes ready to ship. If you wish the great convenience of a credit account, please give us the names of some wholesale firms with whom you have already opened accounts. On receipt of these we shall be glad to enter you on our books as one of our credit customers.

Very truly your

CUSTOMERS GIVING CREDIT INFORMATION

When you are asked to give credit references, give them in as simple and polite a fashion as possible, even if you should think them unnecessary. Here are example answers to requests for references:

Famous Manufacturers, Ltd.
10 Howard St.
Mason City, Ind.

Dear Sirs:

We are enclosing a check for the amount of the goods we ordered on April 12.

Here are our references, so that you may look up our credit reliability before you open a credit account for us: Rogers & Smith, Chicago, Illinois; Mammoth Publishing Company, New York; First National Bank, New City, Iowa.

Very truly yours,

Burns-Brown Corporation
331 Main Ave.
Cincinnati, Ohio

Gentlemen:

Thank you for your letter of the 27th. Since you say that you have opened a credit account for us, we assume that you are shipping to us promptly the goods we ordered, and entering a charge against us for them.

Here are the names of four of your customers who recommended us to you: Continental Hotel, New York; Mayfair Hotel, Chicago; Travelers Hotel, Dallas; Abernathy Hotel Chain, San Francisco.

We have done business with all of these hotels for many years.

Sincerely yours,

Bright Shoe Mfg. Co.
Underhill, Mass.

Gentlemen:

We are enclosing our remittance for $90.00 to cover our order of September 12 for women's shoes—Order 24–8.

You are correct in assuming that we wish to open a charge account with you. Here are the names of three wholesale firms to which you may refer: Conrad & Arnold; Jones and Dupree; Manchester and Bryant. All of these firms are in this city. There should be no delay in contacting them for information.

Yours truly,

The Franklin Store
Chicago, Ill.

Gentlemen:

Mrs. Cleveland Jones wishes me to thank you for your courteous letter.

As both business and personal references I am requested to give you the name of Mr. Roger Fairchild, president of Marshall-Gold Company, and Mr. Oswald Brand, treasurer of Madame Irene, Inc.

In the meanwhile, will you please charge and send the white fox fur coat, size 38, as advertised on page 3 of the Times-Courier.

> Yours sincerely,
> (Miss) Harriett Emmet
> Secretary to Mrs. Cleveland Jones III

Moore and Hood
13 Peach Street
Baltimore, Md.

Gentlemen:

We are enclosing your credit information blank.

We would appreciate it if you could check up on our references within a week. We would like to receive our order in time for our midseason sale.

> Sincerely yours,

ASKING REFERENCES FOR CREDIT INFORMATION

Taylor and Anthony
778 Adams Street
Kansas City, Mo.

Gentlemen:

We have received an application for credit from Mr. Robert Smith who gives your name as a reference. Mr. Smith asked us for credit to the extent of five thousand dollars, for a period of three months.

We should appreciate your giving us such information if you can, including his financial standing, the extent of his business and his reputation for meeting these obligations. We thank you for the favor of your attention.

Yours very truly,

Mr. Joseph Turner
149 Masson Place
Columbus, Ohio

Dear Mr. Turner:

Your name has been given us as a reference by Mr. John Christopher who we understand is a sub-tenant of yours. Mr. Christopher asked us to allow him two months' credit to the amount of one thousand dollars.

We should greatly appreciate your courtesy in giving us information regarding the extent of his business, his financial condition, and his reliability in meeting his obligations.

Yours very truly,

REFERENCES GIVING CREDIT INFORMATION

It is not likely that letters written in answer to credit inquiries would be seen by individuals of the firms under discussion. However, since there is always a possibility that the letters will be seen, the information given should be phrased with considerable care so that there can be no question of libel or lawsuit. If you stick to facts, avoid personalities, and leave out private opinions, you are very likely to be on the safe side.

Beane-Ford Corporation
New London, Conn.

Dear Sirs:

The firm you mention is very well known to us. They have very promptly met their obligations and on several occasions have discounted their bills.

We have not found them quite so prompt when larger sums of money were involved, and we are inclined to believe that they are trying to expand a little more rapidly than their present market safely permits.

Yours very truly,

Randolph-White Company
Denver, Colo.

Gentlemen:

We have occasionally had small transactions with the firm you mention and their payments have been prompt.

Mr. John Christopher and his partner are hard-working, reliable men and have the reputation of trading well within their capital. We believe that you could safely allow the credit you name but we give this information without responsibility, and in confidence.

Very truly yours,

Allen, White & Richards
191 Woodward St.
Washington, D.C.

Gentlemen:

We are glad to be of help to you in connection with your inquiry about Mr. Robert Smith.

Mr. Smith's business is a small one, and we would be surprised if his intake approached five thousand dollars for a three-months' period. We, ourselves, would not be inclined to allow his account to exceed a thousand dollars a month, and would preferably limit ourselves to that period.

Up to that amount we have found it possible to collect what is due us without much delay.

Yours sincerely,

Sentences and Phrases

The firm mentioned in your letter is well known to us.

In answer to your inquiry, we are pleased to report that the firm mentioned——

is respectable and trustworthy. You may safely extend them credit.

is one of the leading firms in this town. Its credit is excellent.

has the highest standing, and an excellent reputation for prompt payment.

is reputed to pay very promptly.

meets its obligations with difficulty.

has a large indebtedness outstanding on our books.

is known to have a very small operating capital.

has a very poor standing.

has the reputation of not paying until it is compelled.

has lost very heavily on recent transactions, and cannot therefore be recommended for credit.

GRANTING OR REFUSING CREDIT

Browning Brothers
881 Willow St.
Toledo, Ohio

Gentlemen:

Thank you for sending us your references so promptly. We communicated with them immediately so that we could get your order to you by the time stated in your letter of July 3.

Replies from the references are highly satisfactory. We now have the pleasure of your name on our books. The merchandise is on its way to you, as requested, F.O.B. San Francisco.

Yours sincerely,

Wallace-Crane Co.
Stonington, Tenn.

Gentlemen:

Thank you for your letter of July 25 furnishing references. We are very sorry to say that they are not satisfactory.

One of the firms named does not know you as a customer sufficiently well. The other reference is quite unsatisfactory.

We are still holding your order, with shipping instructions. If you would please remit the payment we should be glad to send it. We suggest that you wire the money so that we may ship the goods tomorrow.

We may, of course, reconsider the question of credit some time in the future. In the meantime we trust that we can do a satisfactory business on the present basis. We are sending you our new fall catalogue.

Yours very truly,

Willis' Popular Store
Bryant, Texas

Dear Sir:

Thank you for your letter of yesterday giving references in connection with your application for credit. It is with regret that we report these references are hardly what we require.

If you will please refer to our last letter, you will notice that what we ask for are trade references, that is, the names of any firms in our district who have supplied you with goods on credit terms. We are sorry to trouble you again in this matter, but a house policy requires that we have trade references and not personal references alone.

When this routine matter is settled, we expect a very agreeable business relationship.

Sincerely yours,

The Lee Mfg. Co.
2041 Fulton St.
St. Louis, Mo.

Gentlemen:

Please excuse me for having given unsatisfactory references in connection with my request for credit. I thought these would be adequate, to say the least, since they are very well known in the business world. I am, nevertheless, pleased to add the names of the following firms with whom I have accounts: Jones & Heffron, St. Louis, Missouri; Holliday Brothers, Dallas, Texas; Dunby & Son, Chicago, Illinois.

Please look us up promptly so that we may receive the goods we ordered just as soon as possible.

Yours truly,

ASKING FOR PAYMENT IN ADVANCE

Mrs. Washington Smith
Greenville, Pa.

Dear Madam:

Thank you for your order of April 9. We are sorry that we must delay shipping it to you. We are holding the

merchandise in readiness to ship on receipt of your remittance for $47.00.

Since our terms are always cash in advance, we have
no facilities for C.O.D. shipment.

Yours truly,

Mr. W. J. Brown
4140 Wall Street
El Paso, Texas

Dear Mr. Brown:

Your order for six jars of Health Malt received. Apparently you have overlooked the matter of enclosing $4.20
to cover the cost plus the shipping charges. Since ours is
strictly a cash business, we cannot open an account for you.

On receipt of the aforementioned amount we shall ship
the Malt at once.

Sincerely yours,

Terry's Quality Store
Douglas, Florida

Gentlemen:

Ours is a strictly cash business and we have no facilities
for sending goods C.O.D. We hope that the misunderstanding about this point will not be an inconvenience to
you. We are holding your order for twelve pairs of boys'
trousers, Catalogue numbers 4712 and 4714, pending the
receipt of $60.12 to cover the cost and carrying charges.
Thank you.

Yours sincerely,

VIII. COLLECTION LETTERS

Most business firms pay their accounts promptly, so that you don't have to ask them for payment. Sometimes even well established firms pay a few days later, and in such cases there is little need to remind them of their tardiness. If you begin to cry out for payment on the split second, you are likely to give your customers the impression that you haven't much faith in them. It is time enough to write your first collection letter when a few days' grace have demonstrated your courtesy, patience and confidence.

Collection letters are usually written in series.

The first letter is written just to remind the customer that his bill is overdue, and simply and courteously asks for payment.

The second letter is still a reminder, but it is a little more emphatic, tactfully urging payment.

The third letter, written after a considerable waiting period, insists on payment, and is very firm in tone.

The fourth letter demands payment, stressing the fact that you intend to collect even if you have to use your attorney or put the delinquent account in the hands of a collection agency.

The following are collection letters which embody the principles here outlined. First we give examples of each type of letter, then a series that might be used in the collection of one given account.

LETTERS THAT ASK FOR PAYMENT

The *first collection letters* are just reminders that accounts are due. While they are usually not sent out before two weeks following the due date, a longer time is frequently allowed to elapse.

(a)

Dear Sir:

In looking through our accounts we find an amount of $8.00 against you for a January purchase. We are sorry to write to you about such a small amount but we try to get these small balances cleared off early. Will you please send us your remittance?

Very truly yours,

(b)

Dear Madam:

Apparently you overlooked your bill for $60.05 for items purchased during October. It would be a great convenience to us to have your check in full.

Yours very truly,

(c)

Dear Sir:

You have been so prompt in your payment of bills that we are sure you overlooked your January account. The amount of that month's purchases come to $225.00. We hope that you will find it convenient to send us your check for this amount.

Yours sincerely,

(d)

Dear Sir:

$47.50 due January 12

May we call your attention to the above account which has probably escaped your notice?

As your account is a monthly one we should be glad to receive your remittance in settlement at an early date.

Yours truly,

(e)

Gentlemen:

We find that a balance of $92.00 still remains on your account. We would be very glad to have you settle it because we, ourselves, have obligations to meet.

Yours truly,

LETTERS THAT URGE PAYMENT

The second collection letter follows the first one within two weeks or a month, according to circumstances. It underlines the request made in the first letter and is based on the assumption that the customer has simply forgotten to pay.

(*a*)

Dear Sir:

The amount of $8.00 for hosiery purchased in January is still unpaid. As you will recall, our bills are payable the first of the month following the purchase of goods.

Very truly yours,

(*b*)

Dear Madam:

May we again call your attention to the fact that you owe us $60.05 for items purchased during October. You will be saved the bother of additional reminders if you can send your remittance in the enclosed envelope.

Yours very truly,

(*c*)

Dear Sir:

We would like to remind you again that the amount of $225.00 is still due on your January account.

Yours sincerely,

(*d*)

Dear Sir:

$47.50 due January 12

We wrote you on the 24th of January calling your attention to the above account, and we have not yet had the pleasure of an answer from you.

Your account, as noted on our books, is a monthly one,

but we shall be pleased to extend this credit to a quarterly (three months) account which is the limit of credit permitted by our regulations.

Please let us hear from you soon.

Yours truly,

(*e*)

Gentlemen:

We realize that reminders like this are just as much an annoyance to you as they are an expense to us. If you would just remit your small balance of $92.00, we would not have to write you again.

Yours truly,

LETTERS THAT INSIST ON PAYMENT

While the first two letters are polite reminders that the account is overdue, the third letter can begin to get a little tough about things. It should still be courteous, but it must certainly show that your patience is wearing thin.

(*a*)

Dear Sir:

We wonder if you realize just what it costs us to keep writing to you about your January account.

The account is for $8.00 and is considerably overdue. Time and postage for the two statements and letters we have sent you cost us nearly $.50, which is over 6% of your account. Won't you please send us a check by return mail to clear off this small sum?

Very truly yours,

(*b*)

Dear Madam:

Frankly, we are at a loss to understand why you have not communicated with us with regard to your account of $60.05 for items purchased during October.

Perhaps you do not realize that we are willing to accept a part of the payment if you cannot settle it all at once. Why don't you drop in to see our credit manager, Mr. John Abernathy, whom we are sure you will find very sympathetic.

Yours very truly,

(*c*)

Dear Sir:

Perhaps you are not aware of the fact that this is the third time we have had to remind you of your January account. Your indebtedness is for $225.00, which is a large sum to carry this long.

As a routine matter our auditor has asked us whether we wish to place the account in our attorney's hands for collection. We answered that you have been prompt in all past payments and that we did not expect any difficulty with you this time. We hope that our answer was the right one.

Yours truly,

(*d*)

Dear Sir:

$47.50 due January 12

We regret that you have not taken the trouble to reply to our previous two letters about the above overdue account. We must now insist that you send us a check for at least half of this account, say $24.00, by return mail.

We are willing to wait until the first of next month for the balance of $23.50.

Yours very truly,

(e)

Gentlemen:

Our patience is beginning to wear thin. We were quite sincere when we wrote you on April 7 that we do not like to annoy you with letters like this. We are equally sincere when we say that we do not intend to wait very much longer for you to remit your balance of $92.00.

Please let us know which you would prefer: to make an appointment with our credit manager within two days, or to have us place your account in the hands of our attorney for collection.

Yours truly,

LETTERS THAT DEMAND PAYMENT

The fourth letter does not actually threaten suit, since in some instances this threat might be construed as libel. It merely states that you intend to place the account in the hands of your attorney or of the credit agency.

(a)

Dear Sir:

This is the last time we will write you concerning your overdue account of $8.00 for January.

While we would agree that it is not economical to place such small accounts in the hands of our collection attorneys we have the fullest intention of so doing. We have a reputation for courteous service; we also have a reputation for collecting what is due us. We intend to keep both.

Unless remittance comes from you in the nine o'clock Thursday morning mail, we shall ask our attorneys to take over the unpleasant task of collecting from you.

Yours truly,

(b)

Dear Madam:

Why must we write you so repeatedly concerning your overdue account of $60.05 for the month of October?

Why have you not availed yourself of the opportunity to see our credit manager, Mr. John Abernathy?

Why have you not written us concerning your account?

How much longer do you think we are going to wait before we place your account in the hands of our attorneys for collection?

Yours very truly,

(c)

Dear Sir:

We have placed your account for $225.00 in the hands of our attorneys for collection.

We have asked them to wait for exactly five days before proceeding.

Yours truly,

(d)

Dear Sir:

$47.50 due January 12

As you have not replied to our numerous requests for settlements of your long outstanding account, we have to inform you that, unless a check for the full amount is on hand by the 15th of March, the matter will be placed in our lawyer's hands for collection.

We trust that you will see the desirability of avoiding such proceedings.

Yours truly,

(*e*)

Gentlemen:

You might like to know something about the way we handle collections.

We have no formal collection letters which we mail out automatically at certain dates. We take the trouble to write precisely what we mean.

We have just discussed you in a conference with our credit manager and our attorney. Our joint opinion is that unless you remit within three days, our attorney is to proceed. He is already studying the details of the matter. After three days any correspondence from you sent to us will be forwarded to him.

Yours truly,

SET OF COLLECTION LETTERS
Wholesale

(*1*)

Dear Sir:

Ten days ago we sent you a statement of $36.00 then due. We assume that you have not answered because you have overlooked this bill, or intend to pay it later.

We have a large number of small accounts, and it is important for us to receive them on the due dates.

Please send us a check by return post.

Yours truly,

(2)

Dear Sir:

Your account of $36.00 was due on January 7, and we are sorry to remind you that we have had no answer to our letter of January 17 regarding the matter.

The amount is so small that we hope you can send us a check by return mail. This will save us the expense of further correspondence and relieve you of the annoyance of receiving this kind of letter from us.

Yours truly,

(3)

Dear Sir:

In reference to your account of $36.00 for January 7, we have sent you two statements and two personal letters about this account and we have not yet heard from you. We are sure you can see why we will have to draw on you for the amount at the end of this week unless we previously receive your check in settlement.

Yours truly,

(4)

Dear Sir:

You received goods from us on December 9. Your payment was due January 7—in the amount of $36.00. You have not answered the three letters we have written you on this subject. Finally we drew on you, but the draft has been returned unpaid. We have not had a word of explanation.

If you intend to pay but are unable to do so at the moment, you will find us very lenient. However, we have no way of ascertaining your intentions unless you communicate them to us. Please write us within the next four days and save us from the unpleasant necessity of collecting through the courts.

Yours truly,

Retail

(1)

Dear Sir:

This is to remind you that we have an amount of $27.00 charged against you for August purchases.

We like to clear up such items as quickly as possible. Won't you, therefore, send us your check within a few days?

Yours truly,

(2)

Dear Sir:

Apparently you have overlooked your account of $27.00 for merchandise sent you in August.

Perhaps you had intended to pay this on your next visit to our store. Since you might find it more convenient to remit by check, we enclose a stamped reply envelope.

Yours truly,

(*3*)

Dear Sir:

We cannot understand why you have not replied to the letters we have sent you regarding your unpaid account of $27.00. We feel that we have let this run long enough, and expect a remittance within a few days. Otherwise, we regret to say that we may have to take sterner measures.

Yours truly,

(*4*)

Dear Sir:

You are making it very difficult for us to collect the $27.00 due us. We have therefore asked our attorneys to take the matter out of our hands. They will probably not proceed for a few days. If you care to write to us by return mail, you might save yourself a lot of trouble.

Yours truly,

Professional Men and Small Traders

(*1*)

Dear Madam:

I am sorry to remind you that your account is a few days overdue. It would be a great convenience to me if you could settle it within a few days.

Yours sincerely,

(*2*)

Dear Madam:

Ten days ago we wrote to tell you that your account was overdue. It occurs to me that you may not find it convenient to pay the full amount. I find it difficult to make this kind of offer because my expenses are heavy and have to be met every month. However, I should be glad to accept half of the amount now, and half within two weeks.

Please let me know if this is agreeable to you.

Yours very truly,

(3)

Dear Madam:

Even the largest businesses in the country do not like to let credit run more than a few months. I am surprised to find that your account is now four months overdue.

Frankly, I hate to resort to unpleasant means to get the money due me, which I need so urgently. But what else can I do, since my letters to you are unanswered?

Yours very truly,

(4)

Dear Madam:

It would be very easy for you to send me a postcard concerning your overdue account. A reasonable explanation of your delay would probably induce me to let matters wait, although I would find it extremely difficult to do so.

However, since you are apparently not willing to communicate with me, I have decided to enlist the help of my attorney. He has my instructions to proceed unless I hear from you within five days.

Very truly yours,

Debtors' Explanations

It frequently happens that a business man is unable to meet a bill on the day on which it is due. He may have had unexpected reverses; he may be awaiting a check from somebody else; he may, quite reasonably, claim that he does not owe the full amount for which he is charged.

A debtor almost always finds that his creditor is willing to give him extension of time, provided that the debtor makes known his need as quickly as possible and gives a courteous, reasonable and detailed explanation of the situation.

Gentlemen:

I am terribly sorry that we neglected to settle our account which was due on the third of this month.

We have been in such a rush during our recent reorganization that we simply forgot about it.

We are enclosing remittance in full. We thank you for your patience; and assure you that all future payments will be paid on the dot.

> Yours sincerely,

Dear Sirs:

Thank you for reminding us that our August bill is due.

We had depended on a remittance to take care of this bill. We have had definite word that this remittance will arrive in two weeks. May we, then, request that you give us an extension for two weeks' time on our own bill?

> Very truly yours,

Gentlemen:

Replying to your letter of April 28, concerning our account:

We are sorry to say that we cannot send you a check at present for the following reason. Since the opening of our season has been delayed through stormy weather, our customers are still wearing winter clothing instead of purchasing the spring and summer goods we ordered from you.

It is likely that we shall have a change of weather soon which will enable us to realize on the present stocks.

We therefore ask you to do us a big favor. Will you take the enclosed note for sixty days for the balance of the account? If we have any considerable amount of sales before the note comes due, you may be assured that we will send you a check on account.

Very truly yours,

Gentlemen:

In regard to your dunning letter of June 6, we should like to point out the following:

As soon as you take the trouble of adjusting our claim to $90.00 credit on your bill for china smashed in transit, we will send you remittance in full.

Yours truly,

Gentlemen:

How many times do we have to tell you there is an overcharge on our bill? It seems to us that our three letters of explanation are quite sufficient.

Send us a correct bill and we will remit.

Yours truly,

ANSWERING DEBTORS' EXPLANATIONS

Debtors will very rarely take the trouble to write to you, unless they really do intend to pay when they are able to do so. The deadbeat is usually characterized by silence.

When a debtor gives you a reasonable explanation the best thing you can do is to accept it, or perhaps to suggest terms that are somewhat more favorable to you.

If you compel the debtor to sell his goods or other properties at a loss you may lose the opportunity to collect in full, and you may limit the outlet for your goods.

Here are answers to the debtors' explanations just given:

Dear Sirs:

Thank you for telling us that you are expecting a remittance within two weeks. We shall, of course, be happy to grant you an extension of two weeks on your account with us.

Sincerely yours,

Gentlemen:

We quite understand the situation which confronts you. We would like to point out, however, that if you had taken the weather into consideration you would not have gambled on your ability to settle your account on time.

Since the responsibility is yours and not ours, we should

insist on a remittance. You are such a valued customer that we are not going to do this. We suggest instead that you pay one half the amount now. We will accept a note for sixty days for the balance.

May we expect your check promptly?

Yours sincerely,

Gentlemen:

Our claim agent in Hartford makes the following report: Whereas you claim that the china was smashed in transit he finds that it arrived at your shipping department intact. We are enclosing the full details of his report.

This leaves the situation unchanged. Your account for $700.00 is ninety days overdue. We have had enough trouble with this account. Unless we receive remittance within five days we shall place the matter in the hands of our attorneys for collection.

Yours truly,

Gentlemen:

We have just discovered the overcharge on your bill. Our accountant neglected to allow you the usual 2% discount for remitting within ten days last August.

We are enclosing a corrected bill and trust that you will excuse our error.

Very sincerely,

COLLECTION SENTENCES AND PHRASES

Accompanying Statement

We enclose a statement of your account for May.

Herewith is our statement for your October account.

We enclose statement for goods delivered last June.

Reminding Customer of Overdue Bills

We should appreciate your sending check for this amount by return mail, as it is now overdue.

You have apparently overlooked this item, and we trust that you will excuse our asking for a check at this time.

No doubt this small amount has escaped your attention. May we expect an early payment?

If by any chance you have made this payment in the last few days, please disregard this notice. In handling a large number of accounts, we sometimes fall a few days behind in our postings.

The collection of small amounts entails considerable expense. May we, therefore, ask you to remit this amount promptly.

Gentle Reminders

We wish to help our customers as far as possible in the matter of credit, but you must admit that your account is now rather overdue.

We could not possibly sell at such a small margin of profit if all our customers took the extended credit you have taken.

We must really ask you to give the matter your serious attention without delay.

We trust you will see your way clear to send a check by return mail.

Please excuse our reminding you again that you have not yet settled for the goods we shipped you last May.

Letters Urging Payment

The attached bill shows an amount long past due. We would greatly appreciate an immediate remittance.

The account sent you July 7 was due at that time. We have had to remind you of it since then, but we have not heard from you.

You have probably overlooked your account for $35.67 which was due three weeks ago.

I am writing you personally to call your attention to your account of $275.90 which is now two months overdue.

Several requests have been made to you for payment of the enclosed account. We should be glad if you would let us have a settlement, as we are eager to close our books.

This is the second letter reminding you of your bill of $36.86 which was due on June 3.

Perhaps you have overlooked the fact that your account for July purchases has not yet been settled.

We find that our recent letter to you asking you to settle your bill for $5.00 has not been answered.

May we again remind you of the amount due on your account?

We don't like to remind you of your account any more than you like to receive unnecessary correspondence about it. Would it not be to our mutual advantage for you to send us your check for $3.00?

Letters Insisting on Payment

We have carried your account for three months, which is considerably longer than we are willing to do.

We regret to say that we cannot accept any further orders from you unless you settle your account by return mail.

How many times must we remind you of your indebtedness of $76.56 before you are willing to remit?

How much longer must we wait for a settlement of your account?

We should hate to place your account in the hands of a collection attorney. However, unless we receive payment within 48 hours, we shall be obliged to do so.

Our attorneys ask us whether or not we wish to bring suit against you for the amount of your indebtedness to us. We have suggested to them that they defer any action for five days.

Letters Demanding Payment

Unless we hear from you within two days we shall be obliged to give your account to our attorneys for collection.

Unless we receive payment for the above in full by June 3, we shall place your account in other hands for collection.

Since you do not pay attention to our letters you may be willing to listen to our attorneys. We have placed your account in their hands for collection.

We will wait three more days to hear from you. After that, we shall wait no longer. This is final!

Why should we be put to the expense, and you to the annoyance, of collecting the money you owe us? If we have to, we will turn your account over to our attorneys. It would be much pleasanter all around for you to remit today.

Our auditors have called our attention to the credit you are taking. We cannot see our way to allowing it any longer.

Perhaps you think this is just another collection letter, and that we do not mean what we say. We mean every word. And we say that your account will be turned over to our attorneys within five days unless we have a reasonable explanation of the delay.

Debtors' Explanations

We regret that you have found it necessary to write us so often about our account.

Please understand why we have not found it possible to settle our account in full.

Will the following arrangement about our account be satisfactory to you?

Frankly, we have not overlooked your letter asking payment of $45.09.

With regard to your dunning letter, we would like to point out——.

Your letter asking for payment of our July bill has just been brought to my personal attention.

I have pointed out to you that there was an overcharge on your bill.

When you have adjusted our claim, we will remit the balance of our bill.

Answering Debtors' Explanations

We are glad to have your explanation of our overdue account, and we would like to suggest the following terms.

Thank you for pointing out the overcharge in our bill. We are enclosing the new bill.

We are granting you a credit for $56.07 for goods damaged in transit. Will you please remit the balance at your convenience?

Thank you for your promptness in answering our letter of July 3. We are sorry that you are unable to remit, but under the circumstances we agree that it is not possible for you to do so. However——.

IX. PERSONAL BUSINESS LETTERS

The personal type of business letter should be used only when your business relationships are established on such a footing that such letters are perfectly natural expressions. These letters are written to people with whom you have developed friendships rather than to casual business acquaintances. Naturally you should adapt the tone of your letter to the person you are writing to, and should give it just the right degree of formality or familiarity.

GREETINGS

Dear Mr. Jones:

We gladly take off a moment from the business of buying and selling to wish you the very merriest Christmas. I am sure that dealings with you are going to make my own New Year as happy and prosperous as the New Year I wish for you.

Cordially yours,

Dear Mr. Francis:

All year round, I think of you as a friend rather than just as a business acquaintance. This goes double in spades this time of year when I wish you a very merry Christmas and the happiest possible New Year.

Sincerely yours,

Dear Miss Kennedy:

This is to tell you what a pleasure it has been to deal with you this past year. As a small token of my esteem, and as a way of wishing you a happy and prosperous New Year, I am enclosing a desk calendar. As you tear off each page, let it mark another step in our very pleasant relations.

Sincerely yours,

Acknowledgments of Greetings

Dear Mr. Wilson:

Thank you for your good wishes. In reciprocating, let me say that I look forward to a New Year of increasing mutually pleasant business association.

Cordially yours,

Dear Mr. Jamison:

I am glad you think of me as a friend rather than as a business acquaintance, for that is certainly how I think of you. I look forward to seeing you again when you next come to town.

Sincerely yours,

Dear Mr. Sturdevandt:

That was quite the handsomest desk calendar I have ever had on my desk and it certainly was nice of you to send it. As a member of Hampton's Department Store and as an individual, I had always expected the very best from you but this time you really outdid yourself.

Yours very truly,

LETTERS OF CONGRATULATION

It is always a good idea to send a business friend a letter of congratulation when he has done something that merits a verbal pat on the back. You might want to congratulate him for anything from winning a golf cup to winning a bride.

Dear Joe:

It was grand to hear that you are now Personnel Manager, and I know that you are really going places. Your company ought to be congratulated on getting such an able man for the job.

Yours,

Dear Mr. Oglethorpe:

Congratulations on winning the golf tournament. I knew you were a champion Branch Manager but I didn't know you were a champion golfer, too.

Sincerely yours,

Dear Mr. Jones:

Please accept my sincere congratulations on your recent marriage. I was very pleased to read about it in the Dentists' Quarterly. Your many friends in Glenwood join me in wishing you the greatest happiness.

Sincerely yours,

Dear Bill:

You could have knocked me over with a rolling pin when I heard that you married Sally Smith. I have always considered you as one of my very best business friends, but I never thought that anyone I knew personally would have the luck to get a girl like that. My hearty congratulations to you.

Yours,

Dear Mayor Green:

Let me add my congratulations to the many which you are receiving. I am certainly proud and happy to know that you are our new Mayor. We can all look forward to a period of unusual prosperity.

Sincerely yours,

Dear Mr. Beck:

We have just been looking through our books and we find that your branch has established an all-time high for monthly sales of Super Radios.

This is to extend to you and your staff our very heartiest congratulations.

Sincerely yours,

LETTERS OF SYMPATHY

Dear Mr. Johnson:

Mrs. White and I send our deepest sympathy.

Sincerely yours,

Dear Mrs. Chartier:

I was deeply grieved to hear of your recent bereavement. If there is anything we can possibly do for you, please let us know.

Sincerely yours,

Dear Jack:

Although I am not an M.D. I am taking the liberty of sending you the following prescription:

Don't worry about your job, your salary or your work. Take things easy.

I look forward to seeing you as soon as you can comfortably get around.

Sincerely,

Dear Bill:

I certainly was sorry to hear that you had to go to the hospital. The only good thing about it is that you picked a hospital near us so that we can drop in to see you during the noon hour. While you're away from the office we will send your salary to Mrs. Jackson. If there is anything you want and don't let us know about it, you will be fired on the spot. Take warning.

All my best wishes.

Sincerely,

LETTERS OF INTRODUCTION

Dear Jackson:

When I talked to you last Thursday I wasn't able to think of anybody who met your requirements. However, an old friend of mine has just dropped into town, and I think he is just the man you are looking for. Bill Smith did that wonderful sales campaign for Popular Salt in which you were so interested last summer. Enough said. I am sure you will be delighted to talk to him.

Sincerely yours,

Dear Mr. Chelsea:

Mr. J. H. Brown, who will present this letter, is a man I have known for many years. I have always considered him one of the smartest department store buyers of my acquaintance. If there is anything you can do for him, I certainly will be delighted to hear of it.

Yours sincerely,

Dear Frank:

This letter will be brought to you in the little hand of Elizabeth White. She is the young woman I told you about last Friday. You don't deserve to have such a swell copywriter but I like to see able people get a break.

Sincerely,

Dear Mr. Thompson:

The bearer of this letter of introduction is Richard Roe, the son of a classmate of mine. He is seeking an opening in merchandising, and while I know that you do not have anything at present, I am sure that you can give him some valuable information.

I would appreciate anything you can do for him.

Sincerely yours,

LETTERS TO OFFICIALS

Businessmen and others occasionally find reason to write to national government, state or county officials. Such letters should be courteous, brief and to the point, and should always use the correct form of address. In the list that follows, formal salutations are in Roman type; informal salutations in *italic* type.

Correct Forms of Address

THE PRESIDENT	The President of the United States or The President, White House, Washington, D.C.
	Sir: *Dear Mr. President:* *My dear Mr. President:*
THE VICE-PRESI- DENT	The Vice-President, Washington, D.C.
	Sir: *Dear Mr. Vice-President:* *My dear Mr. Vice-President:*

THE CHIEF JUS-
TICE OF THE
S U P R E M E
COURT OF THE
U N I T E D
S T A T E S

The Honorable Harlan Fiske Stone,
Chief Justice of the Supreme Court
  of the United States,
Washington, D.C.

Sir:

Dear Mr. Chief Justice:
Dear Mr. Justice Stone:
My dear Mr. Chief Justice:
My dear Mr. Justice Stone:

ASSOCIATE JUS-
TICE OF THE
S U P R E M E
COURT OF THE
U N I T E D
S T A T E S

The Honorable Owen J. Roberts,
Justice of the Supreme Court of the
  United States,
Washington, D.C.

Sir:

Dear Mr. Justice:
Dear Mr. Justice Roberts:
My dear Mr. Justice:
My dear Mr. Justice Roberts:

MEMBERS OF
THE CABINET

The Honorable, The Secretary of State,
Washington, D.C.

or

The Honorable Cordell Hull,
Secretary of State,
Washington, D.C.

Sir:
Dear Sir:
Dear Mr. Secretary:
My dear Mr. Secretary:

UNITED STATES SENATOR

The Honorable George W. Norris,
The Senate,
Washington, D.C.

Sir:
Dear Sir:
Dear Senator Norris:
My dear Senator Norris:

CONGRESSMAN

The Honorable James W. Wadsworth,
House of Representatives,
Washington, D.C.

Sir:
Dear Sir:
Dear Mr. Wadsworth:
My dear Mr. Wadsworth:

GOVERNOR (STATE, TERRITORY, OR POSSESSION)

His Excellency the Governor,
Albany, New York.
or
The Honorable ———
Executive Mansion,
Albany, New York.

Sir:
Dear Sir:
Your Excellency:
Dear Governor ———:
My dear Governor ———:

STATE SENATOR

The   Honorable ————
The State Senate,
Albany, New York.
or
Senator ———— ————,
The State Capitol,
Albany, New York.

Sir:
Dear Sir:
Dear Senator ————:
My dear Senator ————:

ASSEMBLYMAN
(LEGISLA-
TURE)

The   Honorable ————
————,
Member of Assembly,
Albany, New York.
or
Assemblyman ————
The State Capitol,
Albany, New York.

Sir:
Dear Sir:
Dear Mr. ————:
My dear Mr. ————:

MAYOR

His Honor the Mayor,
City Hall,
New York, N. Y.
or
The Honorable ————
————,

> Mayor of the City of New York
> City Hall,
> New York, N. Y.
>
> Sir:
> Dear Sir:
> *Dear Mr. Mayor:*
> *Dear Mayor ————:*
> *My dear Mr. Mayor:*
> *My dear Mayor ————:*

Letter to the President of the United States

Dear Mr. President:

Your radio address on foreign relations should meet with the approval of all patriotic Americans. It certainly does with mine.

Americans may disagree on national policy, but we should all present a united front in matters affecting the prestige, power, and security of our country.

> Respectfully yours,

Letter to a Senator or Congressman

Dear Sir:

I hope you will support the proposed housing measure. I am sure that you appreciate the importance of such legislation. This measure is not only humane in that it provides healthful living conditions for the workers of the country, but is also good business because it will materially assist building contractors and workers, as well as manufacturers of building materials and supplies. But perhaps the greatest benefit of all is that adequate housing furnishes the right background for better citizenship and a more effective democracy.

Respectfully yours,

Letter to an Editor

To the Editor of
The New York Star,
New York, N. Y.

Dear Sir:

In my opinion the city authorities have a wrong conception of where to effect economy in times of financial stringency. The last place that should be considered for such curtailment is education. And yet education is the first thing to be hit by our city fathers.

Surely there must be many political job holders whose services could be dispensed with, rather than those of teachers who have contributed so much toward the education of the youth of our city.

No economy measures in the public schools of the kind that are proposed can do anything but harm. They will undoubtedly result in the unhealthy crowding of classes, with a resultant lowering of our present standards of instruction. It is not fair to our young people.

I trust that all public-minded citizens and organizations will immediately exert their influence with their councilmen so that the proposed education economy measure will be defeated when it comes up for a final vote.

Very truly yours,

X. LETTERS THAT SELL GOODS
AND SERVICES

The sales letter must first attract the reader's attention, increase his interest, create a desire to possess the goods and finally stimulate him to buy the goods.

Your sales letter should start out with a short and dramatic opening. This can be a simple statement such as, "Prices are going up," "Water is more destructive to your home than fire," "Many women have discovered how to prevent runs in their stockings." The letter can also begin with a question such as "Do you know that prices are going up?" In this case the second part of the letter can answer the reader's curiosity about the question.

In general it is best to write your letter in short, complete paragraphs which make for greater ease of reading.

Write your sales letter just as you would try to win an argument. If you can make your reader say, "Yes, that's true," "Yes, that's true" again, and keep him saying, "Yes" right to the end of the letter he is likely to answer the tacit question "Do you want to buy?" in the affirmative as well.

Keep talking about the product and the customer rather than about "I," "we," "me," "us."

The function of the close of the sales letter is to induce the reader to buy, in other words to "clinch" the sales argument. In most cases the failure to do this would be just like walking away from a prospective customer, saying, "Well, so long," before you took out your fountain pen and tried to get him to sign on the dotted line.

Make the closing of your letter short, clear and strong.

Sales letters can be addressed to the name of the recipient or to a general list, in which case they are addressed, "Dear Reader," "Dear Newlywed," or the like.

GENERAL SALES LETTERS

Dear Sir:

Have you wanted to be "an insider"?

Of course you have. You've longed to know the inside stuff that reporters, columnists, radio commentators, and others are not able to put into their regular stories.

Get back of the scenes with *The Insider!* A weekly ten-page private newspaper that answers the many questions you've been asking about Washington, Labor, Capital, etc.

Send 10¢ for the first 5 issues!

Sincerely yours,

Dear Mr. Ronald:

Frankly, if we made this kind of offer every day or even every week we just couldn't afford to stay in business.

However, we *are* going to make it because we have such faith in our product that we are fully convinced that once you try it you will want to order a full supply.

Our offer is simply this: Please accept the sample of Etho Ink under separate cover with our compliments. If you are not thoroughly satisfied with it, keep it anyway. If you are thoroughly satisfied with it order any amount you like and we will grant you a discount of 50% off our list price. We will take pleasure in filling your order within twenty-four hours.

Sincerely yours,

Dear Madam:

When are peaches in cans not canned peaches?

We are sending you a sample of our peaches in cans so you can tell the difference.

For these peaches in cans have the crisp, firm, fresh, the musky aroma, the suspicion of almond that you enjoy in fresh peaches.

They grow in the Brook Valley where the rich volcanic soil is watered by little silvery creeks which trickle down from Mount Olympia. We pick them carefully by hand, clean them of their golden fuzz, pack them in cans in such a way that they preserve all their flavor.

Try them! Compare them to ordinary canned peaches. And remember our peaches in cans do not cost you a cent more than the other kind.

Yours truly,

Dear Madam:

I was driving by your house the other day and, frankly, your roof didn't look any too safe to me. Of course I couldn't tell from the road, and I didn't want to drop in and interrupt whatever you were doing.

May I come up and see if your roof has any weak spots that the winter rains and snow might find out? I'll do this free, of course.

When a man like me wants to keep in business in a town like this, he has to give people very accurate estimates on things like roofs. That's just in case you didn't take it for granted.

Yours sincerely,

Dear Sir:

It certainly is an inconvenience to go all the way into town every time you want a shirt or some socks or something like that.

But usually you do go into town because you figure that no clothing store in a little community like this would have the quality of goods you want. Well, sir, right there is where you are mistaken. We carry only the finest nationally-advertised merchandise.

We know that you will go to your favorite tailor for business suits and dress suits, so we are not going to stock them. We are going to stock a complete line of haberdashery, sports clothes and accessories.

How about prices? We just moved into a low-rent locality near the station. We spend very little money for advertising and as a result you will find our prices surprisingly low six days a week.

We expect a lot of people to come in and look around without buying anything the first time. We hope to have the pleasure of seeing you soon.

Very truly yours,

Dear Madam:

Have you been busy with paper and pencil figuring how much you need to spend for your summer vacation? You had better revise those figures because you will find it costs you a lot less than you expect to spend a vacation in Holiday House.

Daily rates start at $5.00. That includes meals, FREE golf and tennis, boating, swimming, FREE mountain climbing equipment—everything you need for a delightful vacation. We are right in the heart of the mountains only four hours from New York.

We are enclosing our illustrated booklet and a list of distinguished people who have enjoyed themselves here.

Yours very truly,

Dear Folks:

We are having the time of our lives on Lake Gorney in Maine.

Sometimes we get up before breakfast while the sun is dappling the water and we rush down to the beach for a bracing swim. Then we come back tingling and warm for some of Mother Annie's delicious waffles, sausages and blueberry bread. Other mornings we loaf in bed until nine or ten and let one of the twins tiptoe solemnly into our room with breakfast on a tray.

Talking of food, this is a regular paradise for people who like good things right out of the sea—lobsters, shellfish —and everything else. People have been trying to get Mother Annie to open a restaurant in New York, for years, but she just says, "Why, I just would lie down and die if I had to go away from here."

We can't say that we blame her much. It does something to your soul to live here by the water, listening to the wind sighing through the pine trees, watching the white sails dotting the blue-green water.

There are so many things to do you just don't know where to begin. You can sail the catboats all around the lake, and if you don't know how, Captain Billson can teach you just about as quickly as any man living. If you like speed, you can get in one of the outboard motorboats and you will feel like you're flying. And if you want an all-day exploring or fishing trip, Captain Billson's brother, John, will take you most anywhere you want to go, over to Green Hill, or plumb up to Bangor.

Then there's fishing, hunting, tennis, and golf. We've got a fine library here, too; we've just been loafing in a hammock on the porch where we finished Edith Wharton's "Ethan Frome." There are lots of games in the big recreation room, and the young people dance to a wonderful record-changing phonograph almost every night. Over in Warrentown they've got one of the finest little theatres in the country.

We expected to pay a pile of money when we first heard of Lake Gorney in Maine, but find that it is one of the least expensive vacations we have ever spent.

Why don't you write Mrs. Annie Brown for the full

details? We got your name from a friend. You are just the kind of person she would like to have.

Yours very truly,

Dear Sir:

We have found just the house for you as described in your letter of January 12.

This house has two master bedrooms, a large 18 × 24 living room, pantry, dining room, maid's room.

It's an attractive modern house with great glass windows that offer a beautiful view of the nearby Blue Mountains. The house is in excellent condition and comes with a half acre of attractively landscaped garden.

Please let us know if you want us to open negotiations for you.

Yours very truly,

Dear Mrs. Bennet:

We've found just the apartment you've described to us, and frankly we thought your requirements were going to be almost impossible to meet.

You said that the most important thing was the view, and the view from the living room of this apartment is really breathtaking. You look down onto the Cloverdale Park in which you can see the famous Newbolt Mansion. The river flows just a little to the east and all day long it bears the traffic of boats going northward to the Sound.

And you can see two graceful bridges crossing the waters.

This apartment has not only the view you wanted but the little extra room, too.

We are enclosing a map of the layout. Note that the living room is 18 × 24 feet. The room marked "bedroom" is only 10×12 but it would be perfect for your husband's studio. The larger room, 14×18 feet, is usually used as a dining room but we believe it would make an excellent bedroom. The kitchen is more than ample, and has, of course, the latest refrigerator, electric stove and other electric equipment and improvements.

The apartment is very quiet because no traffic is allowed to travel on the street in front of the house and you are a good distance from the side streets as well as four blocks from the nearest elevated.

The address is one of the best in town.

You will be amazed at the low rent, which is only $90.00 a month. We think this is an exceptionally good buy. Other apartments in the same neighborhood under the same management rent as high as $125.00 a month.

Please let us know if you can see this apartment within twenty-four hours because it will certainly not be on the market very long.

Very truly yours,

Dear Sir:

Life is hard and competition is tough. But Darran Easy Chairs are soft and luxuriously comfortable.

Life in this century sometimes seems shallow, but Darran Easy Chairs are deep.

Sometimes things seem harsh and the world appears to reject you. But Darran Easy Chairs embrace you, relax you, make you look on the brighter side of things.

Darran Easy Chairs fit handsomely into any home. They

have a simple, comfortable-looking construction that fits happily with your furniture.

Under the beautiful, glowing fabrics are concealed specially-constructed pillows over a light aluminum and leather-webbing frame. The chairs are so light that a woman can easily move them from place to place.

Expensive? You be the judge. Darran Easy Chairs start at $35.00. This is possible only because we are manufacturing them in enormous quantities, realizing that they should be the most popular chairs in the country.

Darran Easy Chairs are on display at all better department stores in your city. Just try sitting in one today!

Yours sincerely,

Dear Sir:

Just think! For only 2½¢ each you can keep your name and address in front of every man and woman in this territory. Our Belcraft calendars compel attention beside the finest paintings in your home.

They are reproduced from air brush paintings that glow and gleam in amazing beauty.

A sample has been mailed to you today, and our representative will show you our entire list of 325 samples when he calls on you next week.

Sincerely yours,

Dear Madam:

Many people get the surprise of their lives when they first sit down behind the wheels of a Royal Eight.

One touch on the accelerator, and the Royal leaps ahead

like a frightened jackrabbit, pushing you far back into your seat.

It is thrilling to drive a car with acceleration like this. But do you know what acceleration means in a car? It means rugged power to sweep you over the crest of the highest hill. It means speed to rush you along the roads with the wind whipping your face.

"How I'd love to have a car like that!" we can imagine you saying. "But doesn't it eat up a lot of gas and doesn't it cost a lot of money?"

Madam, the answer is: Not on your life! The Royal is guaranteed to give you a minimum of twenty miles per gallon, and many of our customers report getting twenty-five to thirty miles to the gallon.

Furthermore, the price of the Royal Eight is only $800.00 F.O.B. Detroit.

Probably you have frequently passed the Royal show-rooms at 112 Bond Street, London, Connecticut. Why not drop in today and talk to our sales manager, Mr. Charles Curtis? He will be delighted to take you out for a spin. He will give you a thorough demonstration of the Royal.

If you decide that you just can't do without one of our cars any longer, Mr. Curtis will tell you about our easy payment plan.

Yours truly,

Dear Sir:

Are there any mice in your radio?

Many radios sound like it. Static and other interferences continually heckle the comedian you listen to, disrupt the musical programs and mar the speeches. But when you listen to the Megaphonic you simply don't know that you are listening to a radio. Close your eyes and you can picture the performers in the very next room.

Megaphonic catches every sound—brings you every subtlety of the orchestra.

Why is this so?

The Megaphonic is made with a new built-in construction called the sound trumpet, science's miraculous way of eliminating interference.

Read the enclosed booklet giving you full information about the Megaphonic. Then just phone Mitchell 1300, ask for Mr. Harris, and he will bring a Megaphonic right into your living room.

Listen to any program you like. You will want a Megaphonic.

Yours sincerely,

Dear Sir:

This letter will be dictated, typed, put in an envelope and mailed all within six minutes.

Yes, that's a fact! All this will be done within six minutes flat by the stopwatch.

How in the world is it possible to get out a letter so quickly when, according to our surveys, it usually takes an average of 17½ minutes? All right, we'll tell you why!

This letter is being dictated on a Moderno Electric Typewriter. Don't get us wrong. It's not being taken down in shorthand and then transcribed on the typewriter. It is being dictated directly to the typewriter itself. Because the typewriter is so fast it makes shorthand a thing of the past.

Why, we would like to prove to you that we can train any competent stenographer in your office to take dictation directly on the Moderno Electric Typewriter just about as quickly as you can talk. This means that the Moderno Electric Typewriter can be operated at speeds ranging from 80 words per minute to 140 words per minute.

Remember, everything on the Moderno Typewriter works by electricity: letters, back spaces, carriage returns, tabulating keys. The touch of the Moderno Typewriter is so light that we have sent the following item to the newspaper column, "Believe It or Don't." If a large fly lights on the key of a Moderno Typewriter, it may imprint a letter.

How about letting us bring it in for a demonstration Friday morning? I will call your secretary and see if I can make an appointment with you.

Very truly yours,

Dear Madam:

Here is a little true life story which we think may be interesting to you.

Young Mrs. Whiteside came home one evening last April, left her umbrella in the hallway, and went into the living room to discuss the future with her children.

In most respects that future didn't look any cheerier than the weather outside. Mrs. Whiteside had just come home from the funeral of her husband, Bill. She was left with two small boys to bring up. Never in her life had she felt so lonely and unprotected.

But there was one small ray of hope.

There was something she thought would enable her to

provide for the future, to send her sons to good schools, to support her until the sons had grown to strong men and were able to take care of her.

That, naturally, was Mr. Whiteside's insurance policy. As Mrs. Whiteside went upstairs to look for the policy she thought how good and generous her husband had been—how his every thought had been for her.

Nothing, she knew, could console her for his loss, but his thoughtfulness touched her deeply as she looked through the drawers in his desk, as she touched his diary, his fountain pen, the knife he had had since he was a small boy, the medal he had won in the relay race in high school.

In the desk Mrs. Whiteside found a letter from the insurance company. The letter was a fairly long one, but the point it made was simple. Mr. Whiteside had allowed his policy to lapse.

As Mrs. Whiteside walked down the stairs to her children again, it seemed to take her a thousand years.

Madam, we who deal in insurance would like to abolish from the world all accidents and all sicknesses so that no widow ever again need to face the future without her loved one.

We can't do that, but there is one thing we can do. We can provide you with the tools with which you can carry out many of your dreams for the future, just as you are dreaming them now.

We don't like to call our representatives salesmen; we like to call them advisers. May one of them drop in to see you and Mr. Smith sometime this week to outline our policies? We hope to help you make plans for the future.

Yours truly,

Dear Sir:

There is a policeman waiting for you.

Don't be alarmed. You haven't done anything yet. But a policeman stands near every man who does not know of the laws of the land, for remember "Ignorance of the law is no excuse" for breaking it.

What should you as a businessman know about law? Send for our illustrated leaflet entitled "The Missing Comma That Cost Half a Million Dollars."

Yours very truly,

Sentences and Phrases

In spite of rising prices, we can still offer you substantial savings on wearing apparel.

May we send you a package of our breakfast cereal?

We will pay just the same attention to your needs, whether you place an order of $5.00 or $50.00.

Only those who act right away can have the advantage of this new, reduced price.

Just clip the coupon . . . and watch for results!

Why let your teeth get dull and dingy when it's so easy to make them sparkle!

We are as near as your phone! Just dial Re 4–6709— and we'll be on our way!

May we expect a trial order? Just mail the enclosed card along with $2.00; then we will send the machine at once. Try it for a day, for a week. If you don't find it suitable, return it at our expense, and we will be glad to refund your money.

Try these at my expense. If you are not thoroughly satisfied with them, send back the ones you have not used. You will owe me nothing. I am sure that you will keep them and will want many more. If you want any further information, please call Adams 2–7000 and ask for Mr. Smith.

Just decide on the matter now and you will be more than satisfied later.

We don't wish you to decide until you have tried these automatic razors. Use these razors as you wish for ten days without paying us any deposit whatever. Then you are perfectly free to buy or return them. We rely entirely on your judgment.

Follow-up Letters

There are several kinds of follow-up letters:

Follow-up sales letters which are addressed to those who do not respond to a general sales letter.

Follow-up letters which are sent to old customers whose patronage you want to renew.

Follow-up letters which are sent to customers and prospects in order to announce the arrival of a salesman who would like to call.

Follow-up letters which are sent to dealers in order to enlist their help in a selling campaign.

Sales Letters

Dear Sir:

We have not had the pleasure of seeing you since we announced that we are opening a clothing store near the railroad station.

Perhaps you didn't think it possible that a store in such a small community could offer only the finest sportswear and haberdashery for really low prices.

Don't take our word for it; come in and convince yourself. To make it easier for you we are enclosing a card which will entitle you to a 10% discount during July on anything you buy, no matter how small your order may be.

Yours very truly,

Dear Madam:

"Inexpensive" is a relative word. What is inexpensive for a wealthy person might be very expensive for a person of moderate means.

When we say that you can spend an inexpensive vacation at Lake Gorney in Maine we mean inexpensive for people whose incomes are below $5,000 a year.

Just because we would like to add you to those who have stayed with us summer after summer, we are going to make you a special offer. If you come here for a full two-weeks' vacation we will give you the first two days completely free, including meals, sailing lessons, and a special fishing trip.

Yours very truly,

To Old Customers

Dear Madam:

We were browsing through our records the other day, and ran across your name. "Why," we wondered, "hasn't this good customer been in to see us for so long?"

It can't be because of the quality of our goods, because we know it's right; and it can't be because of our prices, because we know they continue to save people money day after day. You know that if you had any complaints to make about anybody in this store we would be quick to make adjustments.

There is a little bed jacket up in our Junior Miss shop that you would really delight in: Rayon taffeta in a full range of colors—and only $4.50. That's the kind of buy you've been missing.

Please come see us soon.

Sincerely yours,

Dear Madam:

We figure that the washing machine we sold you on May 7 must have saved you about 200 hours up to now.

We hope you are thoroughly satisfied with the washing machine because we use only the finest materials and the best of workmanship just to satisfy discriminating women like you.

Now that you are acquainted with the quality of our household appliances you might like to find out other means we have to save you the time you like to spend with the children, reading, or seeing your friends.

Why don't you come down to our showroom at Maple and Madison Streets, where we have a complete model electric home? It's really one of the most interesting sights you can see.

Cordially yours,

Salesmen's Calls

Dear Sir:

Our Eastern Sales Manager, Mr. Robert McCarthy, is just about to begin his regular spring trip. He will arrive in your city on or about June 15 and will be able to give you a complete description of the office equipment we described in our letter of February 7.

Mr. McCarthy's headquarters will be at the National Hotel, where he will remain for a week.

We sincerely hope that Mr. McCarthy will be of help to you.

Yours very truly,

Dear Mr. Smith:

Since you would find it difficult to come to our factory we are doing the next best thing. We are sending our factory to you.

Our representative, Mr. Bill Hutchins, has been with us for fifteen years, and is familiar with every detail of our operation. He is bringing blueprints and a wide variety of photographs.

Mr. Hutchins is really more of an engineer than a salesman. If he doesn't think that we can help you to solve your problems, he will certainly not try to persuade you that we can.

Mr. Hutchins will be at the Tompkins Hotel in your city from May 12 to May 20 and we will give your secretary a ring soon after his arrival. We hope that you will find it possible to see him.

Yours very truly,

Dealers' Letters

Gentlemen:

After we sent you our price list dated January 12 we found it necessary to increase the price on Item JL-47. Therefore will you please change this from $3.00 to $3.20. We are sorry to trouble you and hope that we haven't inconvenienced you.

Yours truly,

Dear Sir:

Pretty soon everybody is going to be talking about our Wonderflow Fountain Pens.

Our advertising agency has just contracted for space in three national magazines and in two leading newspaper chains. The total circulation will be more than 9,000,000!

This should make our Wonderflow Fountain Pens among the best known in the country.

We believe we have worked out some of the most dramatic and effective sales display material in the field. Our salesman, Mr. Howard, will call on you Thursday with display material. If you will give us your co-operation, we think we can really help you to go to town with Wonderflow Fountain Pens.

Yours very truly,

Dear Mr. Johnson:

A dealer over in Washington County was able to sell $15.00 worth of our Peerless sun glasses in three days. This ought to answer your complaint that Peerless sun glasses don't sell.

We are enclosing a copy of that dealer's letter to show you how you, too, can really make money selling Peerless sun glasses.

Yours very truly,

Dear Sirs:

You've certainly made an excellent showing with our goods, so excellent, in fact, that we wish to help you do even better.

You have such a talent for dramatic display and persuasive salesmanship that we would like to see what you could do with an even greater number of prospects.

Naturally the way we get these prospects is by local advertising.

Some dealers have been so excited about our goods that they have paid for their own advertising space. We don't want you to do that because we recognize that what is profitable to you is profitable to us and we want to bear a generous portion of the expense.

Therefore we would like to make you the following proposition. We will pay fully one-half of the insertion cost of any three of the enclosed advertisements in your local paper. The ads should be run any time between April 1 and June 15. If you can take advantage of this offer please write us at once. We will forward mats of the advertisements for immediate use.

Very truly yours,

Sentences and Phrases

Mr. Jones, our salesman, will drop in to see you within a few days.

If you have decided to try our product, you can place your order with our salesman. He will call on Thursday.

Here are some display signs which others have found highly effective.

We know you are pleased with the table you bought last month. Well, here is a bargain that will delight you even more.

You know there is to be a big convention of Elks in your city in April. How can you reach them? Here is the best way.

May our representative call on you?

I should appreciate the opportunity of calling on you to demonstrate our Supremo machine.

XI. APPLICATIONS FOR JOBS—
AND REPLIES

Answering Advertisements

The letter you write in answer to a want ad has to do a good all-around selling job for you. The safest procedure to follow is simply to set down all the pertinent facts about yourself. The prospective employer will want to know your age, your experience, your background and your references, as well as the remuneration which you have had. Be sure to remember that some detail about your experience which seems unimportant to you may be just the winning detail for the prospective employer.

Here are examples of typical want ads:

Advertising Copywriter—Must have experience on food accounts and ability to write hard selling copy. Married. Age 35. At least 10 years' experience. Salary open. Please write full details, age, experience, accounts handled. Box 27B, Herald.

Phonograph Record Salesgirl—Classical and popular. Experienced. At once. Box 12. Times.

And here are example letters in answer to the above advertisements:

Box 27B
Herald
Dallas, Texas

Dear Sirs:

You ask for a man who has experience on food accounts. Here are the ones which I have handled:

Holliday All-Bran
Ryan's Mustard
Miller's Baby Food
Whimsical Wheaties
LaFollette Milk

You ask for a man who has the ability to write hard selling copy. The two agencies with which I have been connected have made a specialty of coupon returns. On the basis of my record on these returns, I think I can demonstrate to you that my copy is the kind that brings results.

I am married; age, 34.

Enclosed is a record of my work experience.

Yours truly,
William MacDermott

Box 12
Times
Chicago, Illinois

Gentlemen:

In the last fifteen years I have been employed in the Radio and Phonograph Department of the J. Van Alstyne

Department Store, selling both classical and popular records.

I would like to refer you to our buyer, Miss Helen McIntyre, who tells me that I have made an enviable sales record.

In selling records, I found my musical training of considerable value. I studied piano for three years.

I should be glad to call on you at any time you suggest.

Sincerely yours,
Cora Louise Swanson

Here are further examples of letters written in answer to advertisements for jobs.

Dear Sir:

Here are my qualifications for the secretarial position you advertise. My stenographic speed is 160 words per minute, and typing speed 90 words per minute.

I am a graduate of the Interstate Secretarial School where I had training in many business courses other than typing and stenography. I am 35 years of age, and married.

I wish to leave my present position because it does not offer me the opportunity for greater responsibilities which I would expect to find in a firm like yours. My present employer, Mr. George Thurston (Vice-President, Jones & Pratt, investment counsellors, of this city) knows that I am answering this ad.

The following are firms by whom I have been employed in the past. You may write to any of them for references.

Southern Electric Corp., Dallas, Texas.

ABC Publishing Company, Chicago, Illinois.

I should be glad to call on you at whatever time you suggest if you will call me at Boulevard 5–9300, or write me at home, 73 Sands Street, Woodmere, Illinois.

Yours truly,

Dear Sirs:

I was very much pleased to see that you are advertising for a bookkeeper because I have long been interested in your record in the transportation field, and would have applied to you for a position some time ago except for the fact that I have been getting very valuable training where I am.

I think it is now time for me to take the jump. Here are my qualifications: I can keep a full set of books by double entry; controlling accounts; make out weekly and monthly trial balances; make out monthly profit and loss accounts and balance sheets.

I also handle trade acceptances, drafts and notes and see that they are met on due dates.

For the last seven years I have been with Smith & Jones, 21 Pacific Street, of this city. I was in charge of their books all of this time, and I believe I will be given a favorable recommendation.

I am now bonded for $5,000.

As regards salary, I would like to commence at $70.00 per week.

If you will telephone me at Summit 9–2929, I can arrange to call on you at any time the following day.

Respectfully yours,

LETTERS SEEKING POSITIONS

Dear Sirs:

Is it true that you are looking for a rug salesman for your New England territory?

If so, here is something that may be of interest to you. I am selling rugs on the floor of the Jones-Smith Store. The last two weeks I have been keeping a kind of score. I have approached over 300 customers. I have talked to nearly 200. Sixty of those customers have either made purchases or expressed a desire to come back to the store.

Please don't think I am trying to set myself up as a super-salesman, because I am not. But I do know rugs, as I have been in this department for three years. I have also visited a dozen rug factories, and have taken some courses in textile design.

Armed with that equipment, I have been able to make a really effective approach to customers. I like people; I understand people; I know how to help them pick out the rug that will give them the greatest all-around satisfaction, and I have no inhibitions against putting on the pressure when it seems effective to do so.

Yes, I know that there is a great difference between selling rugs on the floor and selling rugs to the trade. But since I have done well in the one, don't you think I might quickly learn to do equally well in the other?

I am twenty-five years old, unmarried, and free to travel.

I will give your secretary a ring Friday morning to see if she will arrange an appointment.

Very truly yours,

Dear Mr. Hammond:

This is for your files. I know there is no position in your office at present, but I should like to be considered when there is one.

I am enclosing a list of my jobs and references.

Yours sincerely,

Dear Mr. Smith:

I know how difficult it is to get good reporters for newspapers published in cities the size of ours. Either you have to train them from scratch, or you have to hire them away from other papers for more money than you want to pay.

That is why I think you may be interested in this application for sometime in the future. You see, I do know the fundamentals of newspaper work because I was for two years editor of my high school paper and for one year editor-in-chief of the Athens University Journal. I have just settled in Zenith with my family. I love this community and I would like to earn my living here.

I am not interested in using The Zenith Herald as a springboard to a job on a bigger paper. I would like to stay with it indefinitely. Because I have a small income, I would be able to start at $15.00 per week, and I would be perfectly happy to begin as copy boy.

I'll drop around to see you Friday afternoon after you have gone to press.

Yours very truly,

Dear Mr. Williams:

Someday in the future you may have need for a new private secretary.

Here is why I should like to offer myself for the job, and here is why I am so much interested in obtaining it. For one thing, I know that you do an enormous variety of work very fast and brilliantly. This offers a real challenge to whoever works for you. It is the kind of challenge I like to meet because, with all due modesty, I have so trained myself in secretarial work that only the most exacting problems are interesting to me.

As to my mechanical abilities, I can take dictation at the rate of 180 words a minute, and transcribe at the rate of 100 words per minute, which won me the Junior Transcribing Championship in Ohio. I taught at the Hooper Business School in Toledo. I covered the subjects of bookkeeping, filing, billing and elementary accounting.

You may wonder why I want to work specifically for you. It is simply that my father ran a small printing business in Toledo and for some time before I left home at the age of 22, I was acting secretary and treasurer of his company.

I cannot, Mr. Smith, think of any job in which I would be so useful as that of private secretary to you, since, in addition to my business training and experience, I could put to work for you and your organization the "know-how" of practical, everyday business handling acquired in growing up in the printing industry.

Yours very truly,

REPLIES TO APPLICANTS

Dear Mr. Jones:

We were very much interested in your letter to us applying for a copywriting position.

Can you come in for an interview on Thursday morning at twelve o'clock?

Yours very truly,

Dear Miss Swanson:

Our buyer, Miss McAllister, would like to see you at eleven-thirty Monday morning, in her office on the seventh floor.

Yours very truly,

Dear Mr. Brown:

Thank you for your letter of April 7. While we are very much interested in your qualifications, we are afraid that you do not quite meet with our requirements.

We thank you for your inquiry.

Very truly yours,

Dear Mr. White:

Our custom is to have applicants for jobs see our personnel director, Mr. Slocum, before he is interviewed by the head of the bookkeeping department. However, we are so much interested in what you have to say about yourself that Mr. John Patton would like to see you right away.

He will phone you for an interview sometime tomorrow evening.

Yours truly,

REFERENCES AND RECOMMENDATIONS

Dear Mr. Rogers:

The bearer of this letter, Miss Helen Jones, has worked for me for six years. She is one of the most able secretaries and bookkeepers we have had. I think you would find her a very valuable addition to your organization.

Yours sincerely,

To Whom It May Concern:

The bearer of this letter, John P. Smith, is one of the brightest young men I have known in advertising. His father was the famous advertising writer, Roger Smith, and Mr. Smith seems well on his way to establishing an equally high reputation in the advertising field.

Mr. Smith has a very unusual combination of qualities. While he is one of the most brilliant and entertaining writers I know, he is also capable of writing very hard-boiled direct mail stuff, and is surprisingly steady and conscientious. Frankly, I think he is a gold mine to whoever employs him.

The only reason I let Smith go was because our billing has been cut down to such a degree that we could no longer afford to keep him. We let several older and more experienced men leave us before we were willing to dispense with the services of Mr. Smith.

Yours very truly,

Dear Mr. Brown:

This will introduce a friend of mine, Richard Roe, whom I hope you can use in your factory. He is one of the most promising young machine tool draughtsmen I have ever met. I know that you will find him intelligent and reliable.

Sincerely yours,

Dear Bill:

This is my secretary, Miss Jane Jones. She is eager to get into publishing, and I know she would be very valuable to a publishing house. She has been very patient with our rather monotonous business here, and I just haven't it in my heart to hold down such an intelligent and ambitious young woman. I can recommend her without reserve for the vacancy you have in mind.

Yours cordially,

FOLLOWING UP REFERENCES

Dear Sir:

Mr. John Morris is being considered for a position with this company and has given your name as a reference. He tells us that he worked with you from 1937 to 1941 in the capacity of sales manager.

We would like you to write us, in confidence, of course, your opinion of Mr. Morris. We want to know what you think of his personality, his ability to get along with his subordinates and his efficiency in obtaining results.

We shall be grateful for your co-operation.

Very truly yours,

Dear Sir:

Mr. Smith has given us your name as a reference. We would like to know how you think he would be able to handle a position as copy chief in our small agency.

In confidence we would like to say that we are greatly

impressed by Mr. Smith's copy and by his delightful personality. We wish, however, to assure ourselves that he will be able to keep up a good, steady level of work, and direct the work of others.

We would greatly appreciate having this information from you as soon as possible.

Yours sincerely,

Dear Mr. Dodge:

Mr. John Monroe has applied for a job with our firm. He has given your name as business and personal reference, saying that he has known you for three years and has been your private secretary for one year.

We would greatly appreciate a statement from you about his personality, reliability, adaptability, etc. We will, of course, consider your reply as strictly confidential.

Yours sincerely,

Replies from References

Dear Sir:

In reply to your letter of January 7, Mr. John Morris was with our company for the past four years. Mr. Morris, we thought, was a very pleasant person who handled his subordinates in a highly successful manner and had a very excellent record of sales.

We cannot recommend Mr. Morris too highly as a sales manager for any company in the field.

Yours truly,

Dear Sir:

Frankly I was surprised that Mr. Monroe gave my name as a reference. If you want to know why, I would suggest that you question Mr. Monroe. You will forgive me if I do not wish to say anything further about him.

Yours truly,

Dear Sir:

Thank you for your letter about Mr. Smith. We agree with you that Mr. Smith is a delightful person and that his copy has plenty of sparkle.

While we did not find him quite stable enough to suit our needs, it is possible that he will show more maturity in a more responsible position. We would suggest that you give him a trial.

Yours truly,

PART TWO

SOCIAL LETTERS

By Edna Ingalls
Formerly of Miss Beard's School and Drew Seminary

INTRODUCTION

To put one's thoughts in a letter neatly and correctly is within the scope of everyone; to write fluently and gracefully is the result of training; to touch the heart of the reader, to make him chuckle, to make words paint pictures that transport another to distant scenes or into the realm of fancy—that is a gift of the gods; but we can all express ourselves kindly, simply, and in good taste. Our written words may be shown to others; they are permanent witnesses of our moods or of our attitude toward life. We can choose to have the tone of our letters cheerful and pleasant. Because one takes time to write, he can add gracious phrases to make the letter an expression of his best self.

The example letters which follow are those of a family and their friends, people living in an average American community, traveling about as pleasure, school, or business takes them. The small boy goes camping; the young daughter is at boarding school; and the older one marries and opens a home of her own. The father and mother plan for them, entertain for them, advise them; and at the same time enjoy their own friends. Here are experiences with which all of us are familiar.

I hope that *Social Letters* will give its readers greater facility and variety in expressing themselves. These letters have been planned to illustrate all the accepted forms used in social correspondence. The headings given in the table of contents indicate exactly where to find the most useful model to follow on any occasion calling for a letter.

E. I.

XII. SUGGESTIONS FOR WRITING
SOCIAL LETTERS

There are helpful hints for writing letters throughout the book, but here in one section are grouped practical suggestions which the reader will want to know.

Writing paper should be of good texture, of a light color such as white and gray, should take ink well, and should always be simple rather than "fancy." Paper with rules should never be used; and envelopes should always match the paper itself.

Letters should never be written in pencil, even to your closest friends. Pen and ink are preferred. However, the growing use of the typewriter has made it acceptable for all informal correspondence.

When you use pen and ink, write as distinctly as you can, leaving generous margins and a good space between the lines. Avoid using inks that are unpleasant to the eye, such as red ink, or that are faded and difficult to read. And when you typewrite, be sure that your ribbon is good and the type faces clean.

When you use stationery that is folded, write on the first and third pages if your letter is to be but two pages long. But if the letter is to be longer, you must follow the natural page order so that the reader won't be confused about the proper sequence of your message.

The address must be clearly written on the envelope, and the letter paper neatly folded, put in the envelope and sealed.

Personal or private messages should never be written on postal cards or post cards. Their use should be confined to brief informal notes.

Always express yourself to the best of your ability when you write a letter. Avoid hackneyed and stereotyped phrases. And in letters to friends, try to write as though you were talking to them.

Additional suggestions for the writing of specific letters will be found in the following chapters.

FORMS OF ADDRESS

Title:	Greeting:
BISHOP (EPISCOPALIAN)	Right Reverend Charles P. Schyler
	64 Lincoln Drive
	Milwaukee, Wisconsin
	Right Reverend:
	Dear Sir:
	or My dear Bishop,

MONSIGNOR   Right Reverend Timothy K. Flannigan
45 East Seventh Street
Valley City, North Dakota
Dear Monsignor:
or Dear Monsignor Flannigan,

BISHOP
(ROMAN
CATHOLIC)   Most Reverend Samuel Winton
28 East Shore Drive
Milwaukee, Wisconsin
Your Excellency:
or My dear Bishop Winton,

PRIEST   Reverend Terrence Riordon
17166 Hayne Avenue
Chicago, Illinois
Dear Reverend Father:
or Dear Father Riordon,

CLERGYMAN   Dr. Thomas P. Lawton
100 Gorham Street
Madison, Wisconsin
My dear Dr. Lawton,
or Dear Dr. Lawton,

Mr. Henry L. Halsey
250 Menona Avenue
Madison, Wisconsin
My dear Mr. Halsey,

RABBI	Rabbi Stephen Winefeld 415 Bergman Street Eau Claire, Wisconsin Dear Sir: *or* Dear Rabbi Winefeld, *or* Dear Dr. Winefeld,
SUPERIOR OF A SISTERHOOD	Mother St. Anaclet, Superior Notre Dame des Bois Trenton, New Jersey Dear Mother St. Anaclet,
SISTER	Sister Patricia Ann St. Joseph's Convent Adrian, Michigan Dear Sister Patricia Ann,

XIII. INVITATIONS, ACCEPTANCES, REGRETS

After the Christmas season, with its activities primarily for the family, is past, Mrs. Hobart feels that she will entertain her friends, some formally, some informally.

LUNCHEON

For a formal luncheon, a hostess writes her invitation on her best note paper and sends it out about ten days before the date set for the luncheon.

> *Mrs. John Colan Hobart*
> *requests the pleasure of your company*
> *at luncheon, on Wednesday, January the seventh*
> *at half-past one o'clock*
> *The Willows*

or the invitation may read as the first one and have the line, *To meet Miss Carey of Prairie du Chien,* written underneath at the bottom of the page:

Mrs. John Colan Hobart
requests the pleasure of your company
at luncheon, on Wednesday, January the seventh
at half-past one o'clock
The Willows
To meet Miss Carey of Prairie du Chien

or:

Mrs. John Colan Hobart
requests the pleasure of your company
at luncheon, to meet Miss Carey, of Prairie du Chien,
on Wednesday, January the seventh, at half-past one o'clock
The Willows

An invitation to luncheon may be extended by writing beneath the name on one's visiting card:

Mrs. John Colan Hobart
Luncheon at one o'clock
Wednesday, January the seventh

A note on one's best note paper conveys an informal invitation:

My dear Mrs. Russell,
Will you give me the pleasure of your company at luncheon on Wednesday, the seventh, at one o'clock?

Very sincerely yours,
Janet Tyler Hobart

The Willows

My dear Miss Hopkins,

Miss Mary Holmes of Rockford is to visit me next week. May we have the pleasure of your company at luncheon, Wednesday, the seventh, at one-thirty o'clock?

Sincerely yours,
Janet Tyler Hobart

The Willows

The responses will be in keeping with the wording of the invitation:

Mrs. Lyman Holcombe
accepts with pleasure the kind invitation
of
Mrs. John Colan Hobart
for luncheon on Wednesday, the seventh of January
at half-past one o'clock

The reply to the invitation written on the visiting card is written on note paper. The reply to the note is naturally a note.

Dear Mrs. Hobart,

I shall be charmed to have luncheon with you on Wednesday at one-thirty o'clock to meet Miss Mary Holmes.

Sincerely yours,
Elizabeth Hopkins

BREAKFAST

An invitation to breakfast will be worded similarly to the one for luncheon, substituting the word breakfast for luncheon and indicating an hour in the morning:

> *Mrs. John Colan Hobart*
> *requests the pleasure of your company*
> *at breakfast, on Friday, January ninth*
> *at eleven o'clock*
> *The Willows*

DINNER

To reply, the guest uses the same type of wording she found in the invitation. If the invitation read: "Mr. and Mrs. John Colan Hobart request the pleasure," etc., then she will reply in the third person:

> *Mr. and Mrs. ————*
> *accept with pleasure*
> *Mr. and Mrs. John Colan Hobart's kind invitation*
> *for dinner*
> *on Saturday, January nineteenth*
> *at seven o'clock*

or:

> *Mr. and Mrs. R. N. Latimer*
> *exceedingly regret that a previous engagement*
> *prevents their acceptance of*
> *Mr. and Mrs. John Colan Hobart's kind invitation*
> *to dinner*
> *on Saturday, the nineteenth of January*
> *at seven-thirty*

To the more informal note one replies:

Dear Mrs. Hobart,

It gives Mr. Latimer and me great pleasure to accept your kind invitation to dinner on Saturday, the nineteenth, at seven-thirty.

> Very sincerely yours,
> Hannah Latimer

If a dinner must be canceled, the hostess will notify her guests at once:

Mr. and Mrs. John Colan Hobart regret that, owing to the illness of Mr. Hobart, their dinner, arranged for next Saturday, must be postponed indefinitely.

The Willows
January 17

The note may be more informal:

My dear Mrs. Latimer:

It is with exceeding regret that I write to explain that the dinner, planned for the nineteenth, must be postponed until the twenty-sixth. One of our cousins from England will be going through Chicago on his way to San Francisco. He has wired us to meet him on the twentieth. I beg that you and Mr. Latimer will give us the pleasure of your company on the twenty-sixth at seven o'clock.

> Very sincerely yours,
> Janet Tyler Hobart

The Willows
January 17

If a person must fill a place at a dinner party at the last moment, the hostess must be very gracious in her informal note to a tried and true friend.

Dear Mr. Brewer,

If you are free tomorrow evening, the fifteenth, will you join my dinner party that has been suddenly upset by the illness of one of my guests? Will you be good enough to overlook the informality of this hurried invitation and to make my husband and me very happy by accepting it? We shall dine at six-thirty in order to be on time for the concert given by the University Glee Club.

Most sincerely yours,
Janet Tyler Hobart

The Willows

A person who cannot accept a last minute invitation to fill in at a dinner must reply by note and give a reason for not accepting. The note should be brief, formal and polite.

My dear Mrs. Hobart,

It is with regret that I cannot assist you to make up the number at the dinner party tomorrow night. A previous engagement will take me into Milwaukee that evening. Thank you for thinking of me.

Yours very truly,
Gerald Brewer

An engraved invitation is written on an unadorned card; a written one will be on the type of initialed or crested note paper the hostess uses.

Sometimes the invitation is a brief written note. Such a note does not imply that the dinner is informal. It contains merely the invitation.

My dear Mrs. Latimer,

We shall be pleased if you and Mr. Latimer will give us the pleasure of your company at dinner on Saturday, the nineteenth, at half-past seven.

Sincerely yours,
Janet Tyler Hobart

The Willows

My dear Miss Thompson,

It will give us much pleasure to have you dine with us on Tuesday, the fifteenth, at half-past six. Afterward, we plan to hear the University Glee Club at the Orpheum.

I hope that you will be able to be with us.

Most sincerely,
Janet Tyler Hobart

The Willows

My dear Mrs. Hobart,

Mr. Latimer and I deeply regret that we are not able to accept your kind invitation for dinner on the nineteenth. I have an appointment for that evening to speak at the state federation of music clubs. My husband joins me in kind regards.

Most sincerely yours,
Hannah Latimer

The note paper is to be folded once into an envelope, which will be addressed to Mrs. Hobart.

When a guest who has accepted a formal dinner invitation finds that he can not, because of unavoidable circumstances, be present, he or she must write immediately on note paper to explain.

512 Lake Road
January 15, 19——

Dear Mrs. Hobart,

Serious illness in the family has made my presence at the house imperative for the coming week. Therefore, I must beg you to excuse me on the nineteenth. The dinner is an event which I was anticipating with the greatest eagerness, but my nephew will need my constant attention for some eight days, the doctor assures me, so I must forego the pleasure of being one of your party. The little fellow is very brave, and with good nursing and watchful care will come through all in good shape.

Very truly yours,
Susan Richards

An invitation to a formal dinner sent out two or three weeks in advance is generally engraved on large cards. The hostess fills in the blanks for the various occasions when she may need them.

> *Mr. and Mrs. John Colan Hobart*
> *request the pleasure of*
>
> *company at dinner*
> *on   , the   of*
> *at   o'clock*
> *The Willows*

They may be written by hand. In that case the invitation will be written on the first page of a double sheet of best note paper.

> *Mr. and Mrs. John Colan Hobart*
> *request the pleasure of*
> *Mr. and Mrs. Herman Latimer's*
> *company at dinner*
> *on Saturday, January nineteenth*
> *at seven o'clock*
> *The Willows*

If the dinner is given in honor of a friend, the invitation may read as follows:

> *Mr. and Mrs. John Colan Hobart*
> *request the pleasure of*
> *your company at dinner*
> *on Saturday, the nineteenth of January*
> *at seven o'clock*
> **to meet Mr. and Mrs. C. K. Foster of Platteville**

THEATER, OPERA, FOOTBALL GAME

An invitation to a theater party is usually written in note form:

My dear Mrs. Hobart,

Will you and Mr. Hobart give us the pleasure of your company on Monday evening, the tenth of February? I shall entertain a few friends at dinner and later at The Blackstone Theater to see Helen Hayes in "Candle in the Wind." We shall dine at six-thirty to allow plenty of time to drive in town and be in our seats for the rising of the curtain.

Very sincerely yours,
Patricia Hewett Marks

410 Forest Avenue
Oak Park
January 26

The Willows
January 28

My dear Mrs. Marks,

It gives Mr. Hobart and me great pleasure to accept your kind invitation for dinner and the theater on Monday evening, the tenth of February. I have not seen Helen Hayes since she played in "Victoria Regina." I understand she gives a splendid performance.

Most sincerely yours,
Janet Tyler Hobart

The following Monday, the daughter was to have the pleasure of hearing Lily Pons in "Lakme." She was happy over an invitation that had come the previous week:

> 1210 Lake Drive
> Forest Park
> February 2

My dear Miss Marks,

Will you give me the pleasure of your company at the performance of "Lakme" at the Auditorium, Monday evening, the seventeenth? We shall be a party of six, including Mr. and Mrs. Murray. If you will be able to join us, I shall call for you at your home at seven o'clock as the curtain rises at eight.

> Faithfully yours,
> Richard Barnes

One of the Delevan girls went to boarding school in New York state. She is invited to see a football game.

> Kemper School
> Danbury, Connecticut
> October 1, 19——

My dear Helene,

May I have the pleasure of taking you to the Army-Columbia game at West Point the twenty-eighth of this month? If you are free to go, mother will write your mother to request the necessary permission from the authorities of your school. Dad and mother will pick me up early in the morning and we shall all call for you about ten-thirty. That will allow us plenty of time for luncheon and to look about a bit at the Academy before the kick-off.

Most sincerely yours,
Grant Short

Saint Mary's Hall
Shrub Oak, N. Y.
October 9, 19——

My dear Grant,

What fun it will be to see an Army game! My mother is willing that I go; so if the red tape starts rolling soon, perhaps I can have permission to be away from school on the twenty-eighth. I hope the Army mule will be in evidence with all his tricks.

Sincerely yours,
Helene Delevan

Formal and Informal Dances

Formal invitations for a dancing party will be engraved on large white cards:

Mr. and Mrs. John Colan Hobart
request the pleasure of your company
at the Lake Ripley Country Club
on Friday evening, January the twenty-fifth
at ten o'clock

Dancing   *R. s. v. p. to*
                                                 The Willows

The replies are in the same manner as the invitation. They will be written on a double note sheet, sealed and sent to Mrs. John Colan Hobart.

Mr. and Mrs. Myron Care Grant
accept with pleasure the
kind invitation of
Mr. and Mrs. John Colan Hobart for
Friday evening, January the twenty-fifth
at ten o'clock
10 Walworth Avenue

Mr. Alfred M. Simms
regrets exceedingly that his absence from town
renders him unable to accept the kind invitation of
Mr. and Mrs. John Colan Hobart for
Friday evening, January the twenty-fifth
at ten o'clock
1050 Kent Parkway

Oftentimes, for informal entertaining, the hostess will send merely the joint card or paper fold and write beneath.

Mr. and Mrs. John Colan Hobart
Dancing at ten.   January the twenty-fifth.
R. s. v. p.

A note for an informal affair is a pleasant and simple way of bidding guests to a dance.

The Willows

My dear Miss Miles,

On next week Monday, the fourteenth, we shall be pleased to have you as our guest to help Ruth enjoy her birthday. Dancing will be from nine-thirty until midnight.

> Most sincerely yours,
> Janet Tyler Hobart

The Willows

My dear Mr. Kent,

In honor of my daughter's birthday, next Monday, the fifteenth, we are inviting a few of her friends to a dance from nine-thirty until midnight. We shall be pleased to have you join us.

> Very sincerely yours,
> Janet Tyler Hobart

An Easter vacation brings two girls home from school. Their mothers plan a dance at the Country Club:

> *Mrs. John C. Hobart and Mrs. Clyde K. Ring*
> *Miss Ruth Hobart*
> *Miss Mary Ring*
> *at home*
> *On Friday evening, April twenty-sixth*
> *at ten o'clock*
> *at the Lake Ripley Country Club*

Fancy Dress

Mrs. Hobart will enclose her visiting card in her share of the invitations and Mrs. Ring likewise, each indicating where a reply should be sent.

For a charity or civic ball, the following form may be used:

> *The honor of your company*
> *is requested by the*
> *members of the Daughters of the American Revolution*
> *at the Lake Ripley Country Club*
> *on Monday, April the twenty-ninth*
> *at ten o'clock*
>
> *Dancing*   *R. s. v. p. to*
> *Mrs. R. N. Latimer*
> *at 50 South Main Street*

ENGAGEMENT

Announcement

The engagement of a daughter may be expressed in formal terms. Each guest at a luncheon may be surprised to find in the fold of the napkin, or on the dessert plate, an envelope containing a card with the following:

> *Mr. and Mrs. John Colan Hobart*
> *have the honor to announce*
> *the engagement of their daughter*
> *Joan*
> *to Mr. John Francis Lacerte*

An informal announcement may be written on cards fastened at the end of ribbons peeking from a centerpiece. The guests at some time during the luncheon will draw the ribbons. A variety of plans can be worked out by brides-to-be.

Good Wishes and Congratulations

Letters from absent friends follow soon. The girl receives the good wishes, the young man the congratulations.

> 3204 Ontario Street
> Oak Park, Illinois
> March 1, 19——

My dear Joan,

The clipping from "The Delevan Gazette" that your mother enclosed in her last letter apprised me of your approaching marriage. My very best love to you, my dear, and the heartiest of congratulations to the fortunate young Mr. Lacerte. Your progress from pinafore days has always been of great interest to me even though we haven't seen each other often, for your mother and I laid great plans for you before you were born. I hope you will find use for the little token of good will I'm mailing you. It carries much love with it.

> Affectionately,
> Janet McKenzie

Dear Joan,

What an occasion the announcement party must have been! I am no end sorry that business duties kept me from wishing you every happiness. Martha wrote me a note, and yesterday I received the clippings you sent. Having the announcements concealed in the corsage bouquets was a clever idea. Most everyone must have been surprised, because you have made up your mind so quickly. Please con-

vey to John Francis my congratulations on having won
the best sport and finest girl I know. May the accompanying little gift be more apt than my adjectives which seem
to be rather trite!

Affectionately,
Susan

Hampton Arms
March 1, 19——

184 Juneau Apartments
March 1, 19——

My dear John Francis,

Congratulations, old man! The news of the announcement made by Joan's mother has traveled fast. You have
won a beautiful and accomplished girl and one that will,
I'm sure, be the best of companions for the future.

Sincerely yours,
Kerwin Johnson

After John Francis and Joan were engaged, the
groom's mother wrote briefly but cordially to Joan.

Château Champlain
Quebec, Canada
March 6, 19——

My dear Joan,

Jean François has written us of the joy that has come
into his life. We want to know you, Joan, and hope that
you may be able to visit us soon. March is a beautiful sunny
month with us when the skiing is at its best. The trails at

Lac Beauport offer sport for the daring and the cautious. The rinks here in the park below our windows afford the best of skating with good orchestras to add to the fun. Bring your snow togs and let us have the pleasure of a visit with you the last week of March.

Dr. Lacerte is writing you a note, too.

Most sincerely,
Marie Lacerte

Château Champlain
Quebec, Canada
March 6, 19——

Miss Joan Hobart
Delevan, Wisconsin

My dear Miss Joan,

Mrs. Lacerte is writing to invite you to visit us the last week in March. I sincerely hope I shall have the pleasure at that time of seeing my future daughter.

Most sincerely yours,
George Lacerte

Because of the great distance to Quebec, Joan was unable to accept the hospitable invitation.

The Willows
Delevan, Wisconsin
March 12, 19——

My dear Mrs. Lacerte,

Your most cordial invitation and kind wishes have been received. It is sweet of you to ask me. Thank you so much, but it is a long, long way to Quebec, and I must stay here at home for the next few months. I do so hope that you and Dr. Lacerte will be able to come here in June. I feel that I know you both; John Francis talks of you so often.

Most affectionately,
Joan

The Willows
Delevan, Wisconsin
March 12, 19——

Dear Dr. Lacerte,

Your very kind note came to me a couple of days ago. It would be a great pleasure to visit with Mrs. Lacerte and you, but I must not leave here now. Skiing and skating are two of my favorite sports. You must be sure to bring Mrs. Lacerte to Wisconsin in June.

Most sincerely yours,
Joan

One of Joan's friends gave a linen shower for her before the wedding, using a calling card to convey the invitation:

Mrs. Jeremy Taylor

Linen Shower for Miss Joan Hobart
June 1, 3 p.m.

WEDDING

Formal Invitations

The wedding invitations may be formal, engraved folded sheets:

> *Mr. and Mrs. John Colan Hobart*
> *request the honor of your presence*
> *at the marriage of their daughter*
> *Joan*
> *to*
> *Mr. John Francis Lacerte*
> *on Saturday, the fifteenth of June*
> *at half past three o'clock*
> *Saint Michael's Church*

> *Mr. and Mrs. John Colan Hobart*
> *request the honor of*
>
> *presence at the marriage of their daughter*
> *Joan*
> *with*
> *Mr. John Francis Lacerte*
> *on the afternoon of Saturday, the fifteenth of June*
> *at half past three o'clock, Saint Michael's Church*
> *Delevan, Wisconsin*

If the church is large and many invitations have been issued, a card accompanies the invitation; and on this is engraved:

Please present this card at
Saint Michael's Church
on the afternoon of Saturday,
June the fifteenth

Mr. and Mrs. John Colan Hobart
request the honor of
Miss Mary Millston's
presence at the marriage of their daughter
Joan
to
Mr. John Francis Lacerte
on Saturday, the fifteenth of June
at three-thirty o'clock
at St. Michael's Church
in Delevan, Wisconsin

Cards to Reserved Pews:

Please present this to an usher
Pew No.
on Tuesday the first of November

Two cards may be enclosed with the invitation:

Within The Ribbons   Within The Ribbons
Mrs. John Colan Hobart   Mrs. George Lacerte

The invitation to the breakfast or reception following the ceremony is engraved on a card the size of

the invitation when folded for the envelope. It matches the paper.

> *Mr. and Mrs. John Colan Hobart*
> *request the honor of*
> *Mr. and Mrs. Simpson's*
> *presence at the marriage of their daughter*
> *Joan*
> *to*
> *Mr. John Francis Lacerte*
> *on Saturday, the fifteenth of June*
> *at half after three o'clock*
> *at Saint Michael's Church*
> *and afterwards at "The Willows"*
> *Delevan*

R. s. v. p.

It may read, "afterwards at breakfast," but not "afterwards at the reception."

Informal Invitations

For a home wedding, those invited to the wedding stay for whatever additional entertainment is given. There is no mention made then of breakfast or reception on the invitation. Sometimes there are no guests at the wedding ceremony.

Mr. and Mrs. Graham Taylor Ross
request the pleasure of your company
at the wedding breakfast of their daughter
Genevieve
and
Mr. Harold Ashley Mason
on Saturday the tenth of June
at one o'clock
at Five hundred and twenty Harrison Avenue

The favor of an
answer is requested.

Use the expression "pleasure of your company" instead of "honor of your presence."

When a wedding is very small and no invitations are engraved, then personal notes are written to the few friends whose presence is desired.

Dear Gretchen,

Wilmer and I are to be married at Saint Michael's Church Monday the eighth at eight o'clock in the morning. We want you to come and afterward to a breakfast on our porch.

Affectionately,
Caroline

A card engraved like the following is often enclosed by the bride to let friends know the future address of the couple.

Mr. and Mrs. Lewis Conklin Brice
will be at home
after the first of November
at 108 Golf View Apartments
Saint Paul, Minnesota

Or a visiting card with the address in the lower right corner will suffice.

Mr. and Mrs. Lewis Conklin Brice

108 Golf View Apartments
Saint Paul, Minnesota

If the wedding is to be a small one for relatives and intimate friends, the acquaintances are often invited to a reception.

Mr. and Mrs. Guy Brooks Hadley
request the pleasure of your company
at the wedding reception of their daughter
Stella Mary
and
Mr. William Gordon Brooks
on Wednesday, the twentieth of June
at four o'clock
Ninety-eight, Garden Road

In the case of a marriage where a more distant relative issues the invitations:

> *Mr. and Mrs. Carl Evans Smith*
> *request the honor of your presence*
> *at the marriage of their niece*
> *Esther Marie Jones*
> *with*
> *Mr. Charles Leslie Taylor*

If R.s.v.p. is put in the lower left corner of the invitation for a wedding at home or of the card extending an invitation to a formal breakfast, luncheon, or supper, a formal reply should be written.

> *Miss Elvira Stephens*
> *accepts with pleasure the kind invitation*
> *of*
> *Mr. and Mrs. John Colan Hobart*
> *for the marriage of their daughter with*
> *Mr. John Francis Lacerte*
> *Saturday, the fifteenth of June*
> *and to the dinner which will follow*

Recalling of Invitations

If a wedding has to be postponed, printed notices on cards are usually sent to those who had received invitations. They may be worded as follows:

Owing to the illness of their daughter, Stella Mary, Mr. and Mrs. Guy Brooks Hadley beg to announce that her marriage has been indefinitely postponed.

or

Mr. and Mrs. Guy Brooks Hadley wish to announce that the marriage of their daughter, Stella Mary, will not take

place on the twentieth of June at Ninety-eight, Garden
Road.

Replies to Gifts

Accompanying the wedding gift will be a calling
card. The letters of thanks for the gifts should follow
within a few days after they have been received. As
they are always sent to the bride, she should acknowledge them in her own handwriting even though she
may not know her husband's friends who sent them.

Dear Mrs. Culver,

The carving set that came to us from you and Mr. Culver is a beautiful one, and I thank you very much for it
and for your thought of us. I hope that I may have the
pleasure of knowing you when we are in our new home in
Milwaukee.

Yours sincerely,
Joan Hobart

The Willows
The eighth of June

My dear Mr. Jacobs,

You have been most kind to send the exquisite tea
service to John Francis and me. I shall be a proud hostess
when I pour tea in my new home, and I hope that you
will be among our first guests at a Sunday afternoon tea
hour on Park Road.

Most sincerely yours,
Joan Hobart

The Willows
The eighth of June

Wedding Announcements

Immediately after the wedding, cards of announcement are issued. These may be a folded sheet similar to the wedding invitation, or they may be large engraved cards.

Mr. and Mrs. John Colan Hobart
have the honor to announce
the marriage of their daughter
Joan
to
Mr. John Francis Lacerte
on Saturday, June the fifteenth
at St. Michael's Church
Delevan, Wisconsin

If there is no near relative to announce the marriage of a widow of middle age, the announcement engraved on notepaper reads:

Mrs. Josephine Gates Murray
and
Mr. Theodore Coates Peak
have the honor to announce their marriage
on Wednesday, the nineteenth of June
at the Cathedral
Duluth, Minnesota

Wedding Anniversaries

For anniversaries:

Hobart—Tyler

19——   *19——*

> *Mr. and Mrs. John Colan Hobart*
> *request the pleasure of your company*
> *on Wednesday, June the twenty-sixth*
> *from four until seven o'clock*
> *The Willows*

CALLING CARDS FOR INVITATIONS

After Joan had been entertained many times as a bride in Milwaukee, she began to repay her indebtedness, using calling cards to convey invitations:

> *Mrs. John Francis Lacerte*
>
> *To meet Miss Emily Sears*
> *March eighth*
> *Tea at four*
>
> *Mrs. John Francis Lacerte*
>
> *Bridge Luncheon*
> *June twenty-sixth*
> *One o'clock*

Calling cards, both for the individual or for the husband and wife, are useful for many occasions:

> *Mrs. John Colan Hobart*
>
> *Wednesdays   The Willows*
>
> *Mr. and Mrs. John Colan Hobart*

This type of card or fold is serviceable for gifts, flowers, calls where condolences are to be expressed, sick calls made, or regrets sent in reply to an invitation to a garden party:

Mrs. John Colan Hobart

Garden party
July Sixth
Four to seven

Mrs. Pembroke of Rockford, Illinois, decided to give a reception to introduce her daughter. She sent out cards, engraved or written thus:

Mr. and Mrs. Esmond Pembroke
request the pleasure of your company
at a reception in honor of their daughter
Eleanor
on Thursday, January the first,
from four till six o'clock
18 River Terrace

If she decides to use another form, the cards may read as follows:

Mrs. Esmond Pembroke
Miss Eleanor Pembroke
At Home
Friday afternoon, January the eighth,
from four till seven o'clock
18 River Terrace

Two or three women may join in giving a reception. In that case the names all appear on the invitation:

Mrs. Esmond Pembroke
Mrs. Carlyle Tainter
Mrs. Nelson Case Holmes
At Home
Friday afternoon, January the fifteenth,
From four till six o'clock
At The Rock River Country Club

If the reception is to be a garden party, then the words, Garden party, appear at the lower left corner of the invitation.

ADDRESSING INVITATIONS

One invitation addressed to Mr. and Mrs. Stephen C. Blake is sufficient for a married couple, one for sisters, addressed to The Misses Baldwin; but separate invitations are required for a mother and daughter, a father and son, or a brother and sister.

REPLYING TO INVITATIONS

A formal reply is in good taste to a formal invitation for an affair where one's company has been requested for a definite date.

Mr. and Mrs. Kenneth Sabin
accept with pleasure
the kind invitation of
Mr. and Mrs. Esmond Pembroke
for Thursday, January the first

A note extending an invitation should be answered by a note, but no reply is necessary when the invitation is a statement of an "At Home" or when an inscribed visiting card conveys the information.

School Functions

At Riverview School where Ruth is a senior, festivities before Christmas vacation are in order:

The Faculty
and
The Class of Nineteen hundred and forty-two
of Riverview School
request the pleasure of your presence
at the
Christmas Play
on Friday, the nineteenth of December
Nineteen hundred and forty-one
at eight o'clock
La Crosse, Wisconsin

R.s.v.p. *Dancing ten until twelve*

The reply follows:

Mr. John Smith Kingsley
accepts with pleasure the kind invitation
of the Faculty and the Class of Nineteen hundred and
forty-two of the Riverview School
for the Christmas play and dance
on Friday, the nineteenth of December

While Ruth was at Riverview, she heard from one of her pals at the University of Wisconsin:

Telephone   Pi Alpha Delta House
Badger 4-6200   25 Butler Court
                                       Madison, Wisconsin
                                       October 26, 19——

Dear Ruth,

We Badgers have a losing team, but a winning spirit— and there's always Saturday night at the Union! November 6 is the Iowa game, Ruth, and I'd love to see you— Do ya s'pose?

                                                    Tom

                          The Sigma Phi House
                        University of Minnesota
                                          November 15, 19——

Dear Ruth,

Would it be possible for you to come up the week end of the Minnesota-Michigan game? There are going to be several parties and I think we could have a swell time.

                                                    Gordon

A telegram came in November:

Gene Krupa playing for Haresfoot dance Saturday. Stop. Can you make it for game in afternoon. Stop. Wire reply.

                                                    Tom

Helene at Saint Mary's in Shrub Oak was having her share of attention, too.

Delta Tau Delta House
Ithaca, New York
January 8, 19——

Dear Helene,

Hope you haven't acquired so much eastern sophistication you'd be bored by a freshman prom. Ours is February sixteenth and I'm looking forward to it—and to you.

And how about bringing a friend for a friend? *He* is six feet, has brown eyes, is good looking and would like *her* to be a blonde—with or without a pug nose.

Do write soon,
Keith

Children's Parties

The children have their party invitations and acceptances to write:

Helen Masters
requests the pleasure of
your company
at a domino party
on the afternoon of July the sixteenth
at four o'clock
10 West Eighth Street

This is sent to Miss Mary Slocum for a little girl and to Master Peter Hobart for a young boy.

Sometimes a simple note written by the child is a good way of familiarizing the young members of the family with the customs of the grown-ups.

Dear Mary,

On my birthday, the tenth of July, Mother is giving a domino party for me. I hope that you can come.

Yours sincerely,
Helen Masters

ANNOUNCEMENT OF A BIRTH

To announce a birth, the baby's card is fastened with a ribbon to the joint card.

Mr. and Mrs. John Francis Lacerte

Miss Agatha Lacerte or *Master Michel Lacerte*

Short notes will be in order as replies to telegrams.

Miss ———

Michel arrived this morning. Eight pounds. Mother son doing well.

In response:

Master Michel Lacerte,

Greetings my boy. Love to you, Mother and Dad.

Ellen Mowbray

A note in response to the announcement of Michel's arrival:

Dear Joan,

Steven and I were so pleased to receive the good news of Michel's arrival. We wish the young man good health and you a speedy recovery. Our heartiest congratulations to the proud father. We are sending a tiny packet with many wishes for the happy future of little Michel.

Lovingly,

Mary

The Christening

As time passes, Joan's little son is to make his first appearance in society at his christening. Joan wishes Mary, a childhood friend, and Louis, a young cousin of John Francis, to be the god parents.

Dear Mary,

Little Michel is to be baptised the first Sunday in August, at St. Bartholomew's Church, at twelve-thirty. You and I were confirmed together. I think it will be exactly perfect if you will consent to be the godmother. Louis Lacerte, a cousin of John Francis, will be the godfather. We plan to have a small dinner party at our house after the service at the Church.

Mother and Dad are driving in for the service and will phone you to ask you to come with them if you would like to do so.

Affectionately,

Joan

Milwaukee
The tenth of July.

Dear Joan,

How dear of you to ask me to assume some responsibility for the future of your precious little Michel. I shall be proud and happy to act as godmother. Your mother called shortly after I received your note, and we shall all drive in together.

Fondly,
Mary

July 14

To acknowledge a gift from the godfather-to-be, Louis, the cousin of the baby's daddy:

Dear Louis,

How proud little Michel will be to have a silver goblet just like his mummy's and his dad's. You know how much we have liked our wedding present. I shall look forward to the day when Michel will be old enough to use his. Let's see, can he manage at three, do you think? John Francis adds his thanks to mine.

Devotedly yours,
Joan

July fifteenth.

XIV. NOTES AND REPLIES

Notes of Congratulation

To congratulate a friend on his success, the note is always proper:

> The Willows
> Delevan, Wisconsin
> January 5, 19——

My dear Carl,

Heartiest congratulations on your election to the office of president of the State Medical Association. Your colleagues have made a wise choice, for if ever there was a man with the interests at heart of medicine and the extension of its benefits, it is you, my dear Carl. May you have a free hand to accomplish your plans!

> Faithfully yours,
> John Hobart

> The Willows
> April 25, 19——

My dear Mrs. Richards,

My congratulations on your appointment to the board of —— in Washington! You are free to go, and the board will profit greatly from your efficiency in organization and from your detailed knowledge of the various phases

of your project. Please accept my best wishes for a successful and happy career.

Sincerely yours,
Janet Tyler Hobart

The Willows
Delevan, Wisconsin
December 3, 19——

Miss Evelyn Thomas
Winona, Minnesota

My dear Evelyn Thomas,

Your second book has just been put on the shelves of our
library. Everyone, I can easily appreciate, will be charmed
with it. The old watchman at the lighthouse is a rare character. He tramps out and back over the rickety boards of
the teetering dock year after year, storing up his homely,
yet wise, philosophy of life. While teaching at Riverview,
did you gather your observations on the young things who
visit the lighthouse? The Indian chants heard at sundown
from Maiden Rock add much local color, and the recollections of the days of the steamers coming to Frontenac
from St. Louis carrying the families away from Missouri
summer heat I liked. The barges, towed alongside, that bore
the coaches, horses, and black servants make us envisage
the picturesque days of yesteryear. "Ol' Man River" has
happy tales to tell of scenes near the headwaters.

I hope this book will bring you much added popularity
as a writer of Mississippi River life.

Most sincerely yours,
Janet Tyler Hobart

A winner in a tournament should be congratulated by friends.

My dear Lennie,

Congratulations on your victory! "Lennie Kingston, Champion, Women's Tennis Tournament, Waukesha County," is going to make a good headline in the morning paper. Such a thrilling match! I wanted to get a chance to speak to you at the club house, but you were so surrounded by photographers and press men that the hoi poloi had no chance. To watch you come from behind as you did, 6–3, 3–6, 7–5, when Barbara Higgins had match point at 5–3, was as breath-taking as it was to listen by radio to the history making Helen Wills-Helen Jacobs Wimbledon classic of 1935. Your friends were vastly more nervous than you were. You seemed the coolest person in the stadium. When you changed courts and gave that characteristic toss of your head, it was as much as to say, "Don't worry. I *won't* let you down." It must have been a happy moment in your tennis career when the president of the association put into your hands the cup filled with American beauties.

How fine it would be if you had time to go into larger tournaments and work your way to Forest Hills. Has Wisconsin ever been represented there?

Best wishes for many more championships.

Ever your friend,

Joan

August 18, 19——

Sometimes a person, unthinkingly, causes another great worry. When Lennie Kingston was playing her match at Waukesha, she had come onto the court wearing her wrist watch. As she changed courts, she tossed it to a girl watching line fouls who went off with it after the match, neither girl having remembered it in the excitement at the end of the tournament.

1128 Juneau Parkway
Milwaukee, Wisconsin
August 18, 19——

My dear Miss Kingston,

Imagine my embarrassment last night when I was taking a handkerchief from my purse to find your watch there! In the midst of the excitement at the end of the match, and in my hurry to get to my car and back to Milwaukee for an appointment, I never once thought of your watch. I hope missing it did not cause you alarm, and that you could remember to whom you hurriedly threw it. I have mailed it to you by insured parcel post and shall keep the receipt until I hear from you that you have received it, safe and sound.

Now that the watch is off my mind, let me congratulate you on your splendid performance yesterday afternoon. It takes a cool head to come from behind like that and ward off two set, match, and championship points. I hope that you may feel next year that you can enter more important tournaments. I am sure you will acquit yourself nobly.

With sincerest wishes for your future success,
Jenifer Tasman

Naturally, Lennie Kingston wrote immediately to Miss Tasman to assure her the watch was in good condition. She enclosed postage to cover the cost of mailing it.

807 Tenth Avenue
Waukesha, Wisconsin
August 19, 19——

My dear Miss Tasman,

Thank you so much for taking care of my watch for me and then for your kindness in mailing it to me. I was conscious of it on my wrist when serving, so I took it off and tossed it to the first person I saw. I am glad it fell into such careful hands. Thank you, indeed, for your congratulations and your wishes for the future. I think maybe my opponent was a little upset by the ball she put outside at the critical moment, for the breaks came my way after that.

Most sincerely yours,
Lennie Kingston

The names of the boys receiving D's for service on the Delevan school football team of 1941 were published in "The Janeston News." As the schools of the two towns had been rivals for years, the players knew each other rather well. One of the Janeston boys wrote to congratulate a friendly rival:

1295 Main Street
Janeston, Wisconsin
January 31, 19——

Dear "Buck,"

In last night's paper, I read that your football coach had presented letters to the squad. Congratulations! You must be mighty proud to have three D's for football. Most fellows have to be content with two or glad to get one. Funny how sentimental people get over these letters they win in athletics. Dad was showing me his high school and college letters the other day. He says he treasures them among his choicest possessions. I noticed he didn't have to go very far down in the old trunk to get them. Then Mother hunted up her basketball letter and numerals. Do you suppose we'll be showing ours to some sons some day? Odd idea, eh?

I notice Mr. Paulson said the football players had the right stuff in them to use against the enemies of our country. We ought to join up and get in some good work together. I never did think much of throwing you to the ground when I could get my hands on you. I'd rather fight with you.

Good luck for graduation.

Your old rival,

Dick

Obtaining an advanced degree is a great event in the life of professional people. Congratulations are in order for a successful student.

My dear Norma,

To think that you have now satisfied a lifelong ambition and can write Ph.D. after your name! My heartiest congratulations! It has been interesting work every hour of each day, I know, and the receiving of the degree shows how you have concentrated during those hours. It takes not only ability, but physical fitness, for it is a great strain. I am so happy you have been able to see it through.

Your plans for a summer at Lac Chabot where you can swim, fish, sleep, and hike with lots of invigorating ozone to breathe sound just right. Little Anne will be there to amuse you, and you may be sure a few of your friends will appear every week-end to share mountain life for a couple of days. You will have new vitality for classes in October. After the year's leave of absence, you must be anxious to return to your beloved campus.

With best wishes for every future success, and with keen anticipation of seeing you in a few weeks,

Most affectionately,
Agnes

Château Champlain
Quebec City
June 30, 19——

Sometimes, applicants for degrees are not successful in obtaining them. Kind friends can help the disappointed person regain her equilibrium.

The Willows
Delevan, Wisconsin
June 10, 19——

Dearest Esther,

A letter from Marian Strong tells me you are in a hospital with a case of frayed nerves. Do stay where you will have good care for a few days until you get your breath again. Then I wonder if I may be fortunate enough to have the pleasure of your companionship for a couple of weeks. Your disappointment over the outcome of the examination is keen, I know, right now; but there will be plenty of opportunities open to you without a master's degree.

Mr. Talbot, of Simonds and Sons, was at the house only yesterday for luncheon talking over some articles he wants John to write on the care of cattle. During the conversation, he remarked that he didn't know what he would do in the autumn, when a woman marries who for five years has helped him get data into shape for publication. He wants a woman who has done graduate work and is familiar with proper forms for bibliographies, footnotes, etc. I spoke of you to him. He seemed pleased and wants to meet you, if you are able, when he comes again, June 26. There, now, isn't that tonic for tired nerves?

I shall be expecting you sometime next week to bask in our June sunshine. Will you like swimming with Ruth and Peter? They like to go over to the lake every afternoon, and I can't always get away to go with them. Summer is my busy season, so I'll be delighted to have company to chat with out of doors when I'm not managing something. This is the prettiest spot in the world to me, and I love all the summer activities with the family at home, their friends dropping in—a game of tennis here, a picnic there, fruit to jell, etc., etc. John says to tell you he'll have the best milk in the dairyland state for you to drink.

Much love, even if in haste,

Janet Tyler

ASKING FAVORS

Longer notes, yet not lengthy letters, form a very necessary part of everyone's correspondence. To ask a favor, to express thanks, sympathy, or congratulation the note with no extraneous details is always in good form. One may use the folded note sheet, a small folded sheet, a single sheet with monogram or crest, or without adornment.

A woman in Prairie du Chien finds she would like assistance from her friend who is teaching at Riverview School:

> 40 Kennilworth Court
> Prairie du Chien
> December 8, 19——

My dear Norma,

A group of ten women in our neighborhood are meeting once a week to knit for the Red Cross. I suggested it might be interesting to have one of the group read or otherwise entertain the others—just to keep us from gossiping all the time. The boomerang has swung true to form. Immediately everyone thought it a capital idea, provided I set the ball rolling and took the first meeting. We didn't want just current events as we hear of those on the radio. It was finally decided to discuss something each country has contributed to civilization. We drew lots for the countries and my slip read, Italy. Would you be willing to send me your postal cards of the paintings and statues that you bought on the trip? I didn't buy many, you remember, as I wasn't in school; but I know you have a representative collection. I think I still remember the arrangement in the Pitti Palace so that I do not need to ask you to place the artists in chronological order. My diary will help me about locations. I shall be so much obliged. I can use a projector, for these good ladies knit as perfectly in the dark as by daylight. You know you may count on me when you want Christmas cookies for those sorority teas you'll be soon sponsoring. Maybe I can thus feel not too much your debtor.

Sincerely yours,
Margaret

The reply:

Riverview School
La Crosse, Wisconsin
December 10, 19——

Dearest Margaret,

It is by return mail that I am answering your cry for help. Gladly do I send you my cards, chronologically arranged, with most important data jotted on the back of each. I hope your group will get as much pleasure from them as my classes always seem to.

I hasten, also, to follow up your suggestion about the cookies. Our tea is to take place the afternoon of the nineteenth. My girls are not in the play this year, so we are responsible for the tea given in honor of parents coming for the play in the evening and to take home their respective daughters after the dance. I like the tea at this season. Girls always look their best in anticipation of the Yuletide festivities. Their eyes sparkle like the snapping hearth fires at the approach of each car under the porte-cochère.

Hastily but fondly yours,

Norma

Gift Notes

A gift came from Joyce Ralston to Agnes Farnsworth, a Latin instructor. The card accompanying it read:

Joyce

With love and congratulations to Agnes

The reply:

My dear Joyce,

The box of chocolates came by the morning mail on my birthday, a very "sweet" reminder of your thought of me. I think you have recalled that Maude Borrup makes my favorite variety. I was pleased to have them to share with three of my friends who came in to play contract that evening.

I expect to start for Quebec Monday, and I shall write you more at length from there.

Most affectionately,

Agnes

After many years of service at Riverview School, Miss Swift, one of the Latin instructors, has decided to leave. Her classes present her with a parting gift:

Riverview School
La Crosse, Wisconsin

May 30, 19——

Dear Miss Swift,

It is hard to tell you with what dismay we learned of your decision to leave Riverview School. Fortunate are the girls who have had the opportunity of finishing their academic work with you. The rest of us can only hope that we shall prove a credit to your training. We all want to express our appreciation of your interest in us and to thank you for the happy hours we have spent in your classes. We hope the traveling case will be useful to you on your trip this summer and a constant reminder of the love and devotion of your students. The classes have paid me the compliment of asking me to write you this note.

Most sincerely yours,
Bettina Bryant

A reply to a gift of flowers sent while Ruth Hobart was in the hospital:

Dear George,

Thank you so much for the gorgeous chrysanthemums. They almost compensated for my not being able to see you win from Stout last Saturday. I may have my first callers tomorrow between four and five.

Sincerely,
Ruth

Dear Mrs. Reynolds,

Such a beautiful African violet plant I have on my bedside table! Thank you so much for thinking of me in such a lovely way. I shall take it to Riverview with me to have in my bay window all winter. I shall hope to have the pleasure of serving you tea some Monday afternoon soon, and then you can note the progress of my pretty plant.

Affectionately,
Ruth Hobart

School Excuses

Notes must often be written to excuse a child's absence at school or to ask some favor of the authorities. Such a note should be written on note paper and enclosed in an envelope which is not to be sealed.

My dear Miss Farnham,

Will you kindly excuse John's absence on Monday and Tuesday? Mr. Kent took him to Chicago to consult an oculist.

Very truly yours,
Mary Tate Kent
(Mrs. E. B. Kent)

25 Mill Lane
March 15, 19——

One day at school, a small boy who had been absent Friday afternoon and Monday morning brought an excuse stating he had been at home with a headache. His teacher questioned him about his indisposition: had the headache lasted that long, had he been at home all the time, had he called a physician? Both she and the principal felt the boy didn't have an excuse that would entitle him to make up his work with full credit. The incensed mother wrote a most hasty and ill considered note, demanding an answer. How much more pleasant an impression she would have made, had she framed the words politely.

My dear Miss Dawson,

Jimmy tells me that you consider the headache he had is not a sufficient reason for his remaining out of school, because he was not confined to the house during the three days. Perhaps he may not have credit for making up the work he missed. You are the judge of that. Jimmy is rather nervous and is troubled with headaches every few months, when the strain of the school room tires him. He recovers more rapidly by playing outdoors in the sun where he forgets school. He is not a very good student as he doesn't like to read; and the fact that he does not recite so well as the other boys worries him, though not enough to make him study. He did not awake Monday in time to go to school, and I did not call him. I realize I should have phoned you or the principal to have avoided the unpleasant situation for Jimmy, but I thought he would not be questioned when he brought an excuse.

The doctor has said previously that his eyesight is normal, and that he is physically in good condition. He frets at the confinement of the long school day until, after a while, his headache is severe.

I shall plan to talk with you at the next P.T.A. meeting if I am not able to get to school to see you before that.

Sincerely yours,
Katherine Kayser
(Mrs. L. O. Kayser)

1814 Eleventh Avenue, South
February 4, 19——

NOTES OF APOLOGY TO NEIGHBORS

A note to a neighbor is often necessary and more gracious than a phone call, especially when the neighbor is not an intimate acquaintance. It also does not permit a reply until the neighbor has had at least a few moments in which to consider her choice of words.

My dear Mrs. Weld,

Unfortunately Scotty has been scratching in your garden and has ruined your pretty pansies. I am so sorry. The Wolfe Greenhouse is dispatching a man to set out new plants for you. We have long talked of enclosing our lawn with a fence. I think we surely shall now and then Scotty will bury bones in his own yard. I hope you will forgive him this time.

Sincerely yours,
Joan Lacerte

My dear Mrs. Kenyon,

I find that Michel has broken a window in your basement. Maybe all little boys have to find out that balls can break glass, but I am sorry it was your window and not ours that he used for his experiment. Max Schliemann, phone 169, does repairing for us. If you will let him know what time it will be convenient for you to have a new pane put in, he will replace the glass and charge the amount on our bill.

Very truly yours,
Joan Lacerte
(Mrs. J. F. Lacerte)

Monday

A Broken Appointment

My dear Clothilde,

Can you imagine my chagrin and confusion when John Francis asked me if I had gleaned any choice tidbits at the club this afternoon? Only then did I remember the meeting and that it was at your home. I am all apologies. Why I wasn't looking forward to it all morning can only be explained, I think, by the fact that Michel was upset. I was so relieved to see a new tooth appearing and to realize I needn't have the doctor that when he took his nap, I promptly had one too and then took him out in his pram for a nice long walk in the sunshine.

I hope you will forgive me and come to my home next week, for I believe it is my turn to entertain.

Most contritely,
Joan

Friday evening

ILLNESS NOTES

When Peter Hobart was ill, his teacher wrote a note:

Room 107
The Lincoln School
February 8, 19——

My dear Peter,

The school nurse tells me you have the measles and must be absent for three weeks. There are several others in the same predicament. You must be careful while you are ill to protect your eyes. Don't think of doing any reading. We'll have reviews when the measley ones all return. Perhaps you can listen to radio programs to help pass the time while you recuperate. The Quiz Kids Wednesdays at seven P.M. are good. I am sending you some conundrums to keep you guessing when you feel well enough to think of some snappy answers.

We all miss you and shall be happy when you return.

Sincerely yours,
Marjorie Tenant

His neighbor pal sends over a note:

Dear Peter,

Mom says you have measles, but aren't very sick. I can't come over to play with you, and you can't come out. I'll bring my feeding station and put it up in the tree where you can see it from bed. Maybe my cardinals will come along. Watch their tails when they spread. The female does a lot more hopping around and comes oftener, but the male is prettier. I'll bet you can't tell the color of the bill of each by tomorrow at ten A.M. Feed them morning glory seeds and cracked corn. They won't eat suet.

Dad has just finished reading "The Prince and the Pauper" to us. Get your nurse to read it aloud to you. Will she do that?

Bud

Peter greatly appreciated the feeding station put up for him by his pal. His period of quarantine had passed more rapidly, watching for the beautiful cardinals and other birds each day. Naturally, after his recovery, he wanted to do something for Bud. Mr. Hobart's suggestion to take the boys to Madison for part of the basketball tournament met with Peter's instant approval. He sat down at once to write a short note to Bud.

Dear Bud,

Dad says he will take you and me to Madison, Saturday, to see Delevan play Oconomowoc in the afternoon, if you can go. I hope your dad will let you. We are to start about a quarter to eleven, have Jones' sausage and cakes for luncheon at the Royce Homestead, see the game, and maybe take a look in the capitol building. Then we'll stop again with Mrs. Royce to have baked ham and sweet potatoes for dinner. I'm going light on food from now till Saturday to have plenty of room for those little pigs. It will all be great if you can go, too. Delevan 20—Oconomowoc 18?

Your friend,
Peter

Wednesday

A letter to an instructor after assistance was given Ruth when ill:

The Willows
Delevan, Wisconsin
November 20, 19——

My dear Miss Swift,

Ruth's letter today has informed Mr. Hobart and me how kind you have been to her, and how much we are in your debt for having helped her to cover the week's translation she missed while in the hospital. You may be sure such interest will be reflected in her attitude toward her work.

I hope you may enjoy "The White Cliffs" that I am mailing you as a slight memento of our appreciation. If Ruth needs more help, will you be willing to give her regular tutoring for a few lessons? When I left, she was making such good progress after her operation that I think she will be back on regular schedule very shortly.

Mr. Hobart joins me in wishing you a happy and successful school year.

Most sincerely yours,
Janet Tyler Hobart
(Mrs. J. C. Hobart)

To a "shut-in" at Christmas, Mrs. Hobart writes:

Dear Mrs. Bennett,

Today when I was selecting Christmas cards for my cousin who is ill, I saw these with the little lambs that I couldn't resist getting for you, thinking of the days we fed the little lambies from the bottle. I hope you have need of these few extra ones.

I am glad to hear from Mr. Bennett that the hospital chart is registering your steady improvement. You will be pleased to know when I dropped in at your home yesterday, the most savory whiffs from newly made bread greeted me. Angie is quite the cook. You will be proud of her.

Mr. Hobart joins me in best wishes for a speedy recovery.

Most sincerely yours,
Janet Tyler Hobart

Condolences

Letters of condolence are generally brief and do not enlarge in detail on the good qualities of the deceased. Such letters are written with the idea of helping the bereaved to live through trying days and not reminding them of a loss they feel very keenly.

A brief note of sympathy:

My dear Susan,

Please accept my sincere sympathy for you in your sorrow.

Fondly,
Mary Walter

315 South Sixth Street
Tuesday

A visiting card, a folder, or a plain card is sent with flowers:

Miss Maureen Scranton

With love and deepest sympathy

A longer note of sympathy:

Dear Susan,

The news of your sorrow has just reached me. Your loss I can realize somewhat, as I know how empty my world seemed when I heard of the passing of your mother. It will be very hard for all of us who knew her well to carry on without her, but we can be glad it was our privilege to have come in contact as long as we did with as lovely a person as your mother. I shall always remember her kindness and her clever witticisms that made week-end parties in your home so charming.

Sincerely,
Martha

Riverview School
Wednesday

Replies may be written any time within six weeks after the arrival of the notes or flowers, or intimate relatives may write the letters acknowledging their receipt.

My dear Mr. Wyckham,

Thank you for the flowers and for the expression of sympathy. Your words of esteem, all of them true, are satisfying to read.

Most sincerely yours,
Thelma C. Grant

My dear Martha,

Your letter and flowers reached me Thursday. Thank you so much for both of them. I shall try to return to school on Tuesday. Will you convey my thanks and appreciation to all the girls who were so kind as to write me.

Lovingly,
Susan

Asking a Person to Appear on a Program

From a near-by town a letter came to Mrs. Hobart requesting assistance on a club program:

318 Doswell Avenue
Fort Atkinson, Wisconsin
December 8, 19——

My dear Mrs. Hobart,

Our book club in Fort Atkinson has asked me to review for the January 15 meeting "I Have Loved England" and "The White Cliffs" by Alice Duer Miller. As you have lived in England, loitered in most of the historic spots and explored many a bosky dell, you know well how to appreciate the foibles as well as the charity and steadiness of the English people. Will you take my place on this program? I hope this request will be a possible one for you to grant, as it seems presumptuous for me to talk about books when you can talk about people. I know, also, that you are an admirer of the work of Mrs. Miller. Many of our club members have visited in the British Isles, so you will have an appreciative group for an audience.

I shall look forward with pleasure to seeing you during your visit to Fort Atkinson and, I hope, to hearing your report.

Very sincerely yours,
Ann Green Cole

My dear Mrs. Tennant,

Unexpected duties in my home will make it impossible for me to take my part on the program for the Women's Club this winter. I am very sorry as I am decidedly interested in the topic assigned to me and should have enjoyed doing the necessary reading. I hesitated to ask anyone to take my place before informing you as you may have someone in mind; but if you haven't, I think Mrs. Wallace may be willing. She has a cousin who has been in Lima on a business mission and has therefore a personal interest in matters Peruvian.

Believe me when I say it is with real regret that I must give up active club participation.

Yours very truly,
Eleanor Page Carey

64 Wentworth Avenue
November 2, 19——

May 14, 19——

My dear Mrs. Hobart,

Ruth has often told me of your visit in England and of the pictures that you brought home with you. In English history class, we have been talking about the buildings and landscape there. Would you be willing to come to school some day next week to tell us about your trip and show us some of your pictures? Our classes are forty minutes in length.

Yours truly,
Cora Strong

The Willows
May 18, 19——

My dear Cora,

Your request to bring cards and speak to the English history class finds me in the midst of a busy week, but it is hard to refuse young people anything when they are in earnest over some project. So you may count on me Friday at two o'clock for half an hour as you suggest. I'll bring some cards and snapshots of rural England, some of the cathedrals and schools, and some of the paintings that hang in the National Gallery, the Wallace Collection, or were at Wembly. The school projector shows these cards satisfactorily as I used it at a P.T.A. meeting last autumn. I am in no sense a lecturer, but if my pictures and descriptions will add to the pleasure of your study, I shall be delighted. It was because I saw some stereoptican pictures of the Passion Play when I was eight years old that I made up my mind I wanted to travel.

Affectionately yours,
Janet Tyler Hobart
(Mrs. J. C. Hobart)

Dear Mrs. Hobart,

Our English history class was delighted and inspired by your talk yesterday. You had to leave so quickly, all we could do to show you our appreciation was to applaud. We hope you will enjoy the lilies of the valley a fraction as much as we did the pictures.

Most sincerely yours,
Cora Strong

May 22

THE NOTE OF INTRODUCTION

The note of introduction is often requested for a friend, never for one's self. A note is dispatched to the friend who will receive the traveler:

Dear Marian,

A friend of mine who has made puppets is on her way to New York City. She has taken a summer course in puppeteering at the University of Washington, has a collection of some fifteen or sixteen, and has given a few shows at the Guild Hall for the entertainment of the children of the Church school. She will be delighted to see Mrs. Hastings' studio if you can arrange to give her a few minutes of your time when you are working there. Her work is solely for her own pleasure and that of her friends. She is not engaged in any commercial pursuit.

Aside from the passion for marionettes that both of you have, I'm sure you will find that you and Margaret Ainsworth, Mrs. Michael Ainsworth, have other interests in common. She is a circler of the globe and knows many of our old haunts in Paris. You will enjoy her.

Most sincerely,
Norma Page

Riverside School
May 8, 19——

A reply:

My dear Norma,

Your letter introducing Mrs. Ainsworth is welcome; for in meeting a friend of yours, I shall be having again a little glimpse of yourself even if by proxy. There are some window puppet shows, for which I have written the script, being presented now at some of the department stores to advertise summer clothes, beach outfits and so on. She ought to enjoy getting behind the scenes for those.

Perhaps we can find a New York version of a Fouquet duck when Arnold has a free night.

As ever,
Marian

Recommending a Girl for a Sorority

Joan has met a girl who she believes will enjoy sorority life at the University and who will have much to contribute to a group that may pledge her.

The Willows
Delevan, Wisconsin
August 16, 19——

My dear Muriel,

While visiting my mother, I have met a charming young girl who expects to enter the University of Wisconsin in September. Knowing that you are always glad to hear of new girls at rushing time, I am sure you will want to add the name of Judy Milnes to your list. She is the daughter of the new rector at Saint Michael's in Delevan, has lived most of her life in Ontario, California, but finished her senior year at Riverview School in La Crosse. She is excellent at badminton. Because I feel sure the Alpha Beta girls will find her congenial, I have invited her to drive to Milwaukee with Ruth and me and hope that you and Katy will have luncheon with us next Tuesday at one o'clock.

Please give my kindest regards to your mother.

Affectionately,
Joan

After Muriel and Katy had met Judy, they notified their rushing chairman at the University about the prospective freshman. Joan soon received a note of thanks for having recommended a new girl.

Wisconsin Beta

of

Alpha Beta Sigma

gratefully acknowledges your recommendation

of Judy Milnes

and wishes to assure you that every courtesy

will be extended to her.

Sometimes the wording on the card may be arranged so that it does not have the appearance of an invitation:

Wisconsin Beta of Alpha Beta Sigma appreciates your recommendation of Judy Milnes and will extend all courtesy and consideration.

Grace Grayman
Rushing Chairman

INVITATION FOR A SHORT VISIT

One may want to send an informal note to an intimate friend to visit at a summer cottage for a fortnight.

Dearest Agatha,

Here Michel and I are, comfortably settled in a pretty cottage on the shore of Mishewawa. John Francis drives out each night—only twenty miles from the office. Can't you and Robin join us for a couple of weeks? We shall so love to have you. We have fresh vegetables and pasteurized Guernsey milk each day from the Hazelnut Farms. The swimming is good. Bob and John Francis can arrange to go back and forth together.

Fondly yours,
Joan

Box 64
Rural Route #3
Waukesha

Of course Agatha is delighted to have the opportunity of getting little Robin into the country under such ideal conditions.

Dear Joan,

Thank you a thousand times for your cordial invitation. Bob will drive us out Thursday. I'll have the car packed full in the morning and then Bob and John Francis can stop for Robin and me at five. I'll have a chicken and dessert ready, so you count on preparing just vegetables that night. Am checking off the minutes until I see you.

Lovingly,
Agatha

Tuesday

A few days after her return to Milwaukee, Agatha wrote Joan a note to thank her for her hospitality.

Dear Joan,

It scarcely seems possible that we are now awaking in a Milwaukee apartment instead of on a screened porch by the shores of Lake Mishewawa. Those two weeks were perfect. Robin gained so much and we're all brown and summery looking now to meet my mother in Rhinelander. Bob and I found a wonderful picnic spot yesterday. When you come back to town in September, we'll hope to have the pleasure of taking you there the first Sunday afternoon.

With best wishes and many thanks from all of us to all the Lacertes,

Agatha

The Week-End and House Party

The week-end or house party is an informal affair to which guests are bidden by note, not by formal invitation. The length of the visit is usually indicated and arrangements made for meeting the guests at the station if they are not coming by motor. Train schedules can be enclosed. An informal verbal invitation, issued some months ahead when friends are together, should be repeated by a written note as the time for the house party approaches and in plenty of time to allow the guest to fit the week-end into her social calendar.

Mutual friends of Mr. and Mrs. Hobart are going to meet at Burntside.

Burntside Lake
Ely, Minnesota
July 30, 19——

My dear Margaret,

The weather reporter has foretold perfect weather for the full of the moon—and a moon is important at a lake. Can you and the doctor join us on our island from Friday until Monday, the 8th–11th? The Indians have their annual dance on their island Friday night, to which we are all invited to come with the customary present of canned goods under our arms. Saturday we have arranged a trip over the portages to Basswood on the Canadian border, and Sunday we'll follow the rangers through their new trail in the forest to see plenty of deer. Tell the doctor to be sure to bring his kodak. We shall be waiting in the launch at the hotel dock to take you right to Blueberry Island. You will ooth be glad to find a shower installed in the guest cabin.

With kindest regards in which David most heartily joins,

Yours as ever,
Patricia

A written invitation to a house party requires an immediate answer containing explicit information about arrival.

My dear Patricia,

You may be sure Curtiss and I shall be delighted to join you at lovely Burntside on Friday the 8th. We shall plan to motor to St. Paul on Thursday so as to break the trip;

the distance from the Lowry to Burntside Lodge dock ought to be covered easily by four in the afternoon. You have mentioned excursions that Curtiss and I both will enjoy to the full. How lonesome we get for the north woods! In my sleep each night, I am snapping deer in their graceful leaps or dancing with "Old Joe" and his numerous offspring.

Curtiss joins me in thanks for your invitation and in kindest regards for you and David.

Most affectionately,
Margaret

Prairie du Chien
August 1

Bread-and-Butter Letters

After these gay occasions are matters of the past, but not of history, "bread-and-butter" or "thank you" letters must come quite quickly, within a week or ten days.

My dear Patricia,

After such a delightful week-end with you at Burntside, I long more than ever for a cabin among the pines and a launch in which to watch the brilliant sunsets of the north. The kodak pictures I believe you will agree are excellent. I think we shall use the one of the doe and fawn for our Christmas card this year. We shall hope for the pleasure of a visit from you and David when you drive back to Chicago in October. The highway along the Mississippi is at its best then and our maples are a glory to see.

Curtiss wishes me also to express his appreciation of your hospitality. With kindest regards from us to you and David,

> Lovingly,
> Margaret

My dear Mr. Cass,

We are inviting five of Ruth's friends to spend the week-end with us at The Willows, July 14–17. Will you join us? There will be a dance at the Lake Ripley Country Club, an informal tea dance at our home, golf, the annual yacht race at Delevan Lake, and as much tennis as you like. We shall hope to see you drawing up under our porte-cochère about four o'clock.

> Most sincerely yours,
> Janet Tyler Hobart

Delevan
July 1

> 16 Crowell Place
> La Crosse, Wisconsin
> July 30, 19——

My dear Mrs. Hobart,

It is with great pleasure that I accept your kind invitation for the week-end of the 14th. I shall plan to drive over on Friday, reaching "The Willows" in the late afternoon, barring mishaps. We have been playing much tennis here this summer, and I'm looking forward to some doubles on your court.

Kindest regards to you and Ruth.

> Most sincerely yours,
> George Cass

The Stevens Hotel
Chicago
August, 19——

My dear Mrs. Hobart,

Before I return to La Crosse and my "pick-up" summer job, I want to mail my letter to you to tell you how much I enjoyed the week end at "The Willows." I asked Priscilla to mail a small box to you—just a little something to remember me by in your very popular household.

Most sincerely yours,
George Cass

25 Longview Terrace
Newport
June, 19——

My dear Dorothy,

Thank you so much for a lovely week end. I enjoyed myself immensely, and feel very much rested and refreshed. Everything was perfect and you are a wonderful hostess.

My love to you and Jack,
Anne

Long Visits

Box 85
Seaside
May, 19——

My dear Ruth,

You are coming to the Pacific coast this summer to visit your cousins in California, my mother tells me. Surely you will be coming by the Canadian Pacific and down the coast in order to see as much of this wonderful western world as you can. Mother and I want you to come to us at Seaside for a week. Daddy will meet your train in Portland and bring you here by auto if you will be sure to arrive on a Saturday morning. Then you can stay here for eight days for a good break in your long train trip, and Daddy will put you back on a Monday train bound for sunny southern California. Have you ever dug for clams or raked crabs from the holes in the sand when the tide goes out? We have beach parties and swim in the pool. The ocean is too cold for me in this section. Mother is enclosing necessary train schedules in her letter to your mother. I do hope you can come. We can exchange all sorts of information about our schools. I imagine my English one in Vancouver differs somewhat from Riverview.

Yours affectionately,

Ann

The Willows
Delevan, Wisconsin
May 25, 19———

Dear Ann,

Such a delightful week and "stop-over" on my trip as you picture in your letter. To say I shall be delighted to see you again expresses but mildly my feelings. Mother and Dad have been studying time tables and maps. They had thought a little of having me travel with two of our faculty by the Sante Fe; but it just happens that friends of ours are making a western trip and going to Seattle by the Canadian Pacific; and they are willing that I join them. We shall stop at Lake Louise on the way. Then they will put me aboard a train for Portland and I can visit you while they see Seattle. Mother is writing all the particulars.

I am checking off weeks and days until the great moment arrives. I shall have material for English themes for all next winter. Will anyone else in my class know how to crack lobster claws? Mother is writing about your family's driving down to Los Angeles to meet us later in the summer when they come out to get me. Let's hope that happens, too.

With keen anticipation, most lovingly,

Ruth

One of the Riverview faculty decided to go to Columbia University to work for her doctor's degree. She wants a friend to visit her over a week end during the Christmas recess.

The Cathedral Residence Club
Morningside Drive
New York City
December 4, 19——

My dear Katherine,

We are making merry over the last week end of this year, because I am taking a little respite from my reading at the library. My dissertation is progressing as rapidly as can be expected, thank you, and will be so much the better, when I view it from a new angle on Tuesday. Can you make your promised visit to New York at this time? We have tickets for "Candle in the Wind" and "Lakme." There is a dance at the Club Saturday night to which a fellow searcher for facts in English history would very much like to take you.

Because I know your love for music, I have accepted invitations for the Philharmonic, Sunday. You will want to hear the boy soprano at Grace Church Sunday morning. You can sleep when you return. That leaves Monday for the shops!

In expectation of seeing you step from the 2:10 train at Grand Central Station, Friday afternoon, the twenty-sixth,

Yours as ever,
Norma

My dear Norma,

Your letter, repeating your kind invitation of last summer, has set my heart to increasing its beats through excitement at the prospect of all the gaiety you describe. I shall plan to arrive on the 2:10 train at the Grand Central Station. I must tell you how very thoughtful it is of you to include "Lakme" in our round of events. I always follow the librettos for the Saturday broadcasts with one of my friends. Now we can compare notes on the advantages of the Metropolitan and the radio. Maybe the future Ph.D. will welcome a vacation from the library, too. My lack of knowledge of English history is appalling, but my rumba is not so bad!

Most sincerely,
Katherine

East Aurora
The twentieth of December

XV. OTHER SOCIAL LETTERS

TRAVEL

Letters from friends on a trip often convey to the reader the joy the writer finds in seeing new sights and making new acquaintances. Perhaps they often sound as though written in a hurry, but most travelers go breezing along without too much time to catch breath.

Château Saint Pierre
Quebec, Canada
August 8, 19——

My dear Joyce,

As I promised after the birthday "thank-you," here is the "letter of later date" from Quebec. The French summer session, for English speaking students, at Laval University closed Saturday; and some day this week the doctor, Marie-José, and I plan to start on our annual trip in Gaspésie. In the interim a few words to my friends. With Abbé Maheaux as lecturer, a group of students visited the Hotel Dieu. The nuns very graciously opened their gardens for us. They have the house of the habitant, the Indian wigwam, the "voiturette de fleurs" still in the gardens as reminders of the tricentennial celebration of 1939. In their museum they have much old silver, pewter, beautifully embroidered vestments that were brought by the priests and nuns who came in the seventeenth century. The rare old editions and records in the library really interested me more. Some of the "religieuses" live in the old, old section of the building. The part for the patients is most up-to-date. One evening, one of the students gave a piano recital for them in their reception room, an exquisite musical evening to which I was indeed fortunate to be invited. The nuns came in to take seats behind the grille. Abbé Savard referred to them as "les roses blanches."

I liked visiting the Ursuline convent where young French Canadian girls have studied during three centuries. "Les Dames Ursulines" have given their students a love of study and an appreciation of the finest in literature, music, and art to judge by the character of the women who were, as little girls, entrusted to their care. They must have been stern mistresses, too, for Marie-José tells of having to kneel for many an hour on the floor of the chapel because of some breach of discipline.

The drives along the Saint Lawrence, on the Island, out to Lac Beauport, or in the Laurentians are picturesque. We sang "A la Claire Fontaine" all through the woods. A bit of the customs of bygone centuries is always to be seen on the Island. The processions at Corpus Christi time are impressive. I like to hear the men sing as they march along the roads bordered by small evergreen trees. The children in white carrying banners are earnest in their devotion.

From generation to generation, they pass on their heritage of French Catholic civilization. From Mother Marie of the Incarnation have come, even to the present day, the virtues and heroic leaven of courageous ancestors. Truly, they are a valiant and devout people!

From Ste. Anne des Monts or Percé, I'll drop you a card to let you know how the cod tastes this year, and whether we have seen whales spouting.

Affectionately yours,

Agnes

Bon Voyage

Sailing off on a ship is probably the most thrilling beginning for any trip, as the setting is picturesque. It can't help but be. The stewards, the loading of baggage, the long dock, the graceful ship, the gangplank, the shining deck and cozy cabins, the variety of good looking strangers most of whom will be at least speaking acquaintances by the end of a week— some much more—the band playing "The Star-Spangled Banner," all set one's blood a tingle, to say nothing of the anticipation of new adventures in foreign lands. A railroad station just hasn't the oomph! Will these scenes of embarking for beloved foreign ports be ours again? With the belief that they surely will be, I shall include a few notes to be received on board ship and to be dispatched by the ship's pilot and from the arrival port. Mrs. Hobart and Joan sailed from Montreal one June. No "Star-Spangled Banner" from there, but "God Save the King."

Many gifts, expressions of good will for a "bon voyage" were awaiting them in their cabin. Books, flowers, a basket of fruit, each bearing a card with a short inscription, "Best wishes for a good voyage," "With the compliments and good wishes of——," "With love and best wishes for a 'bon voyage.'" Right away, they found a place at a desk in the writing salon to pen a few notes of thanks to be taken by the pilot's boat at Quebec.

THE MONTROSE
CANADIAN PACIFIC LINES

June 10, 19——

Dear Dad,

The flowers are beautiful. Mother and I will enjoy them at our table for several days, I know. Everything is so new and so exciting. I heard several French Canadians singing their songs as they stood on the stern waving to some friends on the dock. I shall watch for Jeanne de Guise and Gabrielle as we go past the Convent at Sillery. They wrote they would ask the Mère St. Anaclet if she would walk with them to the border of the grounds to wave at us. It is like a foreign land already. I'm all anticipation for the summer to come.

Love, and thank you for the wonderful trip and the flowers,

Joan

The Montrose
Canadian Pacific Lines

June 10, 19——

My dear Philip,

The roses are beautiful. I have one on my coat lapel now. The others will brighten our table and maybe our spirits if the boat begins to rock! I'm sure this is to be a wonderful summer with so propitious a beginning.

Most sincerely,
Joan Hobart

A few people from Quebec had come out on the tender to bid them Godspeed. Brief notes, sent from Liverpool, were happily read by their friends whom they had left on this side.

The Montrose
The Canadian Pacific Line

June 17, 19——

My dear Monique,

How kind it was of you to come aboard at Quebec to wish us "Bon voyage." It is too bad you couldn't have made the trip with us. We've had very good weather and scarcely anyone has missed meals. We've had movies, a concert by all the talented people, deck tennis and golf, a fancy dress party, countless card games, and some French every afternoon.

Your friend, Jean François, or John Francis as he is known among the English people on board, has a good baritone voice. He has sung "Alouette," "A la Claire Fontaine" and "Il était un Petit Navire" on all occasions and at the concert had everyone in the salon joining with him. He suggested we dress as "Tweedle-Dum" and "Tweedle-Dee" at the costume party. You should have seen me holding a pillow case, slipped over my head, my arms crossed over my head. That case reached to my waist. A steward's coat was fastened over a cane attached to my belt. Eyes, nose, and mouth cut from Hershey bar wrappers and pasted on the pillow case supplied the features for my long face. Jean François was dressed similarly. We danced together, with others, and were in the grand march although we couldn't see a thing. And were my arms tired when it was time for unmasking! But next evening we were given prizes, very graciously presented by Lady Clyde. Mine was a silver jewel box adorned with the Montrose crest.

By the way, do you know that Jean François is a graduate of Cornell and now has a position in Milwaukee? Of course you do.

Last night we stood in the point of the prow to watch the ship's progress among the islands. The lights from the buoys flashed on and off as our course took us to the north of Ireland. This noon we sailed up the Mercy to disembark at Liverpool. Such commotion among stewards to get us to "paste our labels," have passports ready, line up for the immigration inspector, etc., etc.

Oh, I forgot to tell you, Jean François asked when I inadvertently dropped my watch on the deck, "Does it still walk all right?" I told him it ran in the busy U. S. A.

I shall hope to find a letter from you somewhere in Europe. You have my itinerary.

Affectionately,

Joan

After a trip, conducted by a travel bureau, previous strangers often become very good friends; others who have taken kodak pictures along the way wish to exchange with those who have also had good success with snapshots. After her trip west, Ruth found she had some very clear views taken at Lake Louise and at Glacier. She sent some prints to a woman who had had a berth across the aisle.

The Willows
Delevan, Wisconsin
September 4, 19——

My dear Mrs. Manson,

Did you have a wonderful summer? I hope so. Looking over my snapshots at my leisure brings back many of the high spots of the summer, not the least of which was the trip through the Canadian Rockies. Will you share a few recollections with me?

Best wishes to you for many more pleasant trips.

Most sincerely yours,
Ruth Hobart

HOUSEHOLD AFFAIRS

Letters written to settle household affairs and among members of a family are important factors in one's daily life.

The second maid at "The Willows" decided she had lived on the outskirts of town long enough. She wanted to be nearer the bright lights, so Mrs. Hobart wrote her a letter of reference:

Kaia Dahl has been in my service as second maid for six years. She is neat and efficient, and pleasant in the home. On some occasions she has cooked for us for a few days at a time. Her waffles are delicious, and she knows about a sizzling steak.

I should have been glad to retain Kaia, but she prefers now to work in town. The fact that she has been in one position six years is a recommendation in itself.

> J. T. Hobart
> (Mrs. John Hobart)

To the new "hired" man, employed to help the tenant, Mrs. Hobart writes a note:

Mrs. Hobart wishes Frank to curry Topsy, the black saddle horse, before nine in the morning. The bridle needs a bit of attention.

Before arriving home after a trip of a month's duration, she drops a note to the cook to notify her of their coming:

Dear Olga,

Mr. Hobart, the children and I expect to arrive Tuesday, about noon. Will you plan a dinner for 12:30 and get something that can be kept hot; roast, scalloped potatoes, new squash, aspic or molded salad and fruit for dessert.

Be sure to have something in the house for a light supper; maybe cream soup, cheese soufflé and preserves and cookies.

Mr. Hobart asks me to say the thought of one of your soufflés makes his mouth water now.

J. T. Hobart

March 28, 19——

To the New Rector

Mrs. Walter Milnes
Rectory of Saint Michael's Church
Delevan, Wisconsin

My dear Mrs. Milnes,

To be away from Delevan and not able to join in the welcome Saint Michael's parish is extending to its new rector and his family is one of the drawbacks of being away from home this winter. There are occasions when it would be so delightful to be in two places at one time. However, I hope I shall soon have the pleasure of calling on you. I feel sure you will enjoy Delevan. It is a very pretty town, and Saint Michael's parish is an active one.

Mr. Hobart joins me in extending our best wishes to you and Dr. Milnes for a happy life with us at Saint Michael's.

Most sincerely yours,
Janet Tyler Hobart
(Mrs. J. C. Hobart)

FAMILY AND INTIMATE FRIENDS

To a Daughter Away at School

April 2, 19——

Dearest Ruth,

This has been a busier week than usual after our six weeks away. You were your usual thoughtful self in having a letter here to greet me. Thank you, dear. My hasty note informed you of our arrival. The house was in spic span order and both Nora and Anna smiling in greeting. There are five new kittens, hard cats, no Persians this season; four white collies, the prettiest, softest, fluffiest ones we've ever had it seems to me; a little staggering colt; seven or eight Guernsey calves that are demanding the care of an expert like your father; there are lambs, no bottle babies among them as yet; and altogether the spring seems a very successful one. There are crocuses up in the front lawn. Tulips, hyacinths, and jonquils will be on their way soon. We ought to have some spring gardens worth seeing when you arrive Easter Monday. I have a new cretonne slip cover for your room with tulips cocking saucy heads at you. Peter is likely to be stuck in the mud with his pony. They are so happy to be together, they are exploring every corner of every field.

Last night we had the pleasure of having Dr. and Mrs. Milnes and four children dine with us. They are delightful people. Peter and Jim are even now sworn pals. Judy is having a real problem in school. Mrs. Milnes didn't want to leave her in the west alone to finish her senior year's work, but she is simply lost here, with no Latin beyond the sophomore year and no French. She is a good student. I read a little of the Aeneid with her last night and spoke French with her. I talked with Mrs. Milnes about the idea that was fomenting in my brain immediately—"Ulysses fertile in resources!"—and the upshot is that I phoned Dr. Kenyon to see about a scholarship. Judy will be with you tomorrow if all works out. Now, Ruth, will you be a committee to see that she doesn't get lonesome the first day? She will make friends right away, I know, and will give you girls some stiff competition in class. She has pretty brown hair and merry eyes, but I can see she has been worried and unhappy over her school work.

No more now, my dear. Your father will be driving to La Crosse for you in a couple of weeks if he can. Your friends that I have seen, Cora, Betty, Tom, Hazel, Bill, all send their kindest regards. Roller skates are all over the sidewalks in town.

With love,
Mother

The Daughter Asks for Advice

Ruth writes from Riverview for advice.

Dear Dad,

I am in a great quandary. To take them or not to take them! That is the question. Put the college board exams for the object, and my uncertain future for the reason for my indecision and you get a fair picture of my mental attitude. If I go to the University of Wisconsin where I do not need a record in examinations, there is no reason to go through the strain and stress of writing them; and I shall be perfectly happy at Wisconsin and certainly have excellent courses from which to choose, especially should I take history, science, or journalism. The historical library is second only to Harvard's, I understand, and the lecturers the finest to be found, all of them truly scientific historians. There is no place where one has more fun along with work than at Madison. I'll have a grand time there, Dad. Then, on the other hand, I seem headed for the classics and modern language! I can specialize in that, too, at the University. And yet why have I studied so hard to prepare for the exams if I side-step them at the end? Do you think there is any likelihood of my going to Westminster? I'm glad I've studied to learn all this stuff. It seems useful or usable. What shall I do?

In most profound perplexity,
Ruth

April 4

Dear Ruth,

Your letter shows that you are giving serious thought to the arrangement of your future and that your type of training is bearing fruit. I can see that there is no doubt in your mind about taking the examinations. That's as it should be, and there need be no worrying over writing an examination the substance of which you know. It is rather an opportunity for seeing how well you can handle your tools that you have been learning to use. I like to have you well grounded in the literature and philosophy of other centuries and of other countries than our own. You have thereby an excellent standard by which to judge what you meet that is new and ofttimes called modern. You have time while you are young to do the drill work. You can read Latin, French, and English literature with appreciation. I hope you will soon be able to know Homer and Sophocles in the original. Your mother and I will help you start this summer. You can branch into the field of history and geography. You will enjoy travel and can meet people of other lands with a sympathy for their background. Because you know literature, you will love music and art. That is one reason for my having entered you at Riverview. I am glad you have an appreciation whether you acquire an ability in execution or not. I believe that in our new world there will be great opportunities for young people without prejudice.

I shall be happy to have you study at Westminster and meet young women from other sections of our country. When you are a little older, I think you will be able to assimilate better the advantages of University work with the broadening influence of the masculine point of view. At sixteen you may be moved by the cut and color of a professor's tie more than by the truth of his utterances!

Good luck to you in your examinations and may the readers of the papers feel as sure as I do of your ability to handle your material. Your Latin vocabulary is good. You speak French easily.

Your affectionate

Dad

April 7

From a Young Son at Camp

Camp Minnieska
Lac Court d'Oreilles
August 8, 19——

Dear Dad,

This camp is great. Yesterday I caught a muskelunge. Well, at least I brought it up to the boat. I felt a jerk on the line, reeled in, saw Mr. Muskie jump and then pull the line out spinning. I reeled him in again. Oh, he was a big, handsome one. He jumped and jerked, and put up a lot of tricks. He made the reel fly so fast, it took a piece right out of my first finger. The last time I brought him to the boat, Mr. Hawkins shot him. Eighteen pounds he weighed, and we had muskie steak for supper with blueberry muffins. The Indians know how to cook fish. They roll it in corn meal, Jake, our guide, says. I should like to have sent the fish home to you and Mother; but I have eaten so much of the others' fish, I was glad to have one to offer. I think, anyway, bass will suit the size of our range better, and they are good. I'll bring some.

But, Dad, may I stay another week? I'm learning a lot here. I think it would be beneficial. Please let me.

Your loving son,
Peter

The Willow Farm
August 12, 19——

Dear Peter,

To have you like Court d'Oreilles is very good news to me. I have spent some of my best vacations fishing in those waters, and I can taste your muskie steaks in retrospect. This time, Peter, I think we must limit the outing to two weeks. You are needed here for some chores while the men are harvesting. Do not be too disappointed, for I have another surprise in store for you. How would you like to go north to Burntside with me at partridge season? After the farm is put in shape for the winter, I can get away for a week, and I had planned to take you with me in October, provided, of course, your grades in school are averaging B+. You can compare the north woods of Minnesota with Wisconsin's timber lands.

We'll be expecting you in a few days, then. The new cider is tiptop this year. The Duchess apples were never better.

Your loving

Dad

Between School Friends

Burntside Lake

Ely, Minnesota

October 15, 19——

Dear Bob,

Burntside is a lake you must see some day. There are bears here. One came down a Norway trunk right by my window this morning. There are deer in the swamp a half mile back of the cabin. All the cabins up here built by the Finnish people are of Norway logs. No nails are used.

To get to the hunting: We have an Indian guide who has taken us across our arm of the lake and over a portage. There we have found partridge perched on the limbs of the trees, sitting on rocks or scurrying off the path. Partridge are stupid things. I've been in a car and seen a partridge sitting on a fence. There he sits while the driver stops the car, gets out, puts his gun together and shoots. In cold weather a partridge will conceal its head in a hole near the root of a tree, presumably to keep warm and let its exposed body freeze. Partridge are easily prepared. And are they good to eat! Partridge with corn and wild rice is a supper for a king or a hunter. The Indians boil their birds and have stew, but we wrapped each one with a couple of strips of bacon and cooked them in a large iron skillet.

You and your dad will have to plan to come here next open season.

Your pal,
Peter

When Peter was camping at Burntside Lake, the little dog that had been loaned him for company got into difficulties with a porcupine. Peter had to take him into town to the veterinary, but as he found no one at the office, he had to leave a note:

Friday afternoon

Dear Dr. Thompson,

Will you call me at the Parkman residence, 182 J, as soon as you return? My dog, Bob, has quills, in his muzzle, that I can't extract. When I heard the commotion behind the cabin, I found the "porkie" with his nose between the logs, his pink eyes showing his fright. Bob was dancing around him, barking. I lured Bob in the cabin with a piece of meat and started taking out the quills. All around his mouth they were thick. Then he opened his mouth and several had lodged in his throat and the roof of his mouth. He was very quiet while I took out those. The ones in his nose have hooked themselves in. He needs your attention as soon as you can take care of him.

> Hastily yours,
> Peter Hobart

When Ruth was spending a few days camping on the Red Cedar River with a schoolmate from Menomonie, she wrote a note to her mother to share some of her good times with the family:

> Menomonie, Wisconsin
> August 15, 19——

Dear Mother,

Such a good time as I'm having, camping with Eff and her friends at "Buzzard's Roost" on the point! Naturally, we practically live in bathing suits. We swim, we follow this winding river upstream and downstream, across little lakes made by the dams put in by the old lumber company or the new electric power company. One dam was constructed just last year, so the water has only recently risen to any height. We were paddling our canoes yesterday among the tops of trees and could reach out and bring branches with birds' nests right up to us. It seemed like a fairy land setting on a stage. We dive out the end of a row boat, swim awhile, then climb back in. We dry out while eating luncheon in some pretty spot.

Every evening we have a bonfire around which we sing

songs. The girls' boy friends from town usually drop in to see us when the "Uncle Sam" makes its evening trip. That is the barge, paddle wheel in rear, that churns up and down the river every night, twice on Sundays, and other times by appointment for a dozen passengers. It will accommodate fifty or seventy-five easily. We brought all our camp supplies on it. The water is deep enough at our dock for it to pull alongside. Last night Eff's parents had come to pay us a visit and to bring another baked bean for the larder. After the barge was part way to town, we all thought it would be fun to row in for ice cream. Eff and I were at the oars. We took the row boat so as to take all five. We began to gain on "Uncle Sam." As we came nearer, we saw all the passengers watching our race. We drew up about even as we left the river channel and started to cross the little lake at the town. Eff's father called to us that he'd treat us all if we reached the pier before the barge. Eff is on the crew at Milwaukee Downer, so she was in practice for distance rowing. We hoped our strength would equal our enthusiasm. You understand "Uncle Sam" can go only so fast—which speed isn't great, but it can keep it up. On we went, one of the girls at the rudder counting strokes for us and the other two singing to keep time for our rhythm. We really felt ourselves pulling away. The people on "Uncle Sam" sent up a shout as we outdistanced them. Then we tied up at the pier and helped Mr. and Mrs. Berwick step off their boat as it wheezed a last wheeze. Did that ice cream taste good! I'm sure a regatta on the Thames or Hudson could mean no more to the strokesman or cockswain of a racing shell than our race did to us for a few minutes.

Thanks so much for the food you sent. It arrived safely and quickly disappeared.

Much love to you, Dad, and Peter,
Ruth

Saint Mary's Hall
Shrub Oak, N. Y.
November 1, 19——

My dear Ruth,

Sally writes me that you are in the hospital. An appendix can be disquieting no longer than its term of connection with the human body, so yours is likely to be inefficient from now on. Defenestrate the horrible thing! I heard that word over the radio the other night, so I want to get it into my vocabulary immediately. Have you started studying for scholastic aptitude tests? We are having vocabulary work in English, Latin, and French.

The best bit of this term has been the Army-Columbia game. The cadets came marching on the field with swinging step, they sang, cheered, threw their caps in the air, broke ranks and ran for their seats. Their cheer leaders, I'm sure, were members of the gymnasium team. They executed somersaults, hand springs, cartwheels in perfect rhythm. The mule and a little mule with blankets of blue and gold were ridden by cadets, not in uniform. Every time there was a touchdown, the mules galloped the length of the field in front of the bleachers. Between halves the Army band was on the field. Such thrills. The game was great, the score went 7–6, 13–13, 19–20, 27–26, ending in the Army's favor. There is nothing that quite equals the choir's singing of "The Corps" and "Alma Mater."

I am sending you William Saroyan's "Aram Is My Name." It's the most laugh provoking book I know at present. Will the nurse read it to you?

I hope you will be entirely recovered for Christmas vacation. Oh, you will be—in six weeks you will have forgotten you ever had an appendix. I'll help you with Aeneas and try to speak French if you have to make up lessons.

Affectionately,
Helene

Riverview School
La Crosse, Wisconsin
December 5, 19——

Dear Helene,

Thank you so much for Aram. I'm sure, laughing over his getting into the Presbyterian choir helped cure me at a rapid rate. His physical test sent us into gales, too. That makes good reading for a hospital patient.

No sooner was I back at school than I was deep in plans for the Christmas party. There is a tea given in the afternoon for the parents and guests who arrive early, a lovely dinner just for the students, the chapel service for everyone, a short play, most always of a religious nature, and then the dance. One society has charge of the tea, one of the play, and the other of the dance, so no one is overly rushed.

If the weather is good, Mother and Dad will drive up for me. But if the radio announces storms for Friday and Saturday, I go home by train.

I shall be so anxious to see you and to hear about your festivities. The last three days I was in the hospital, Miss

Swift came up an hour each day and translated my Latin lessons to me. It was surprising how much I remembered when it came to our tests. Mlle. took me the first Monday after my return and told me in French the story of what I'd missed, so there was just English and Math to do, and that seemed to fit in all right. We have the finest teachers at Riverview. No lessons to do in vacation, therefore, but I want to review with you. Those college boards do loom bigger and bigger on the horizon.

Much love,
Ruth

Asking a Friend to Act as Chaperone

My dear Mrs. Stevens,

Five girls at Shrub Oak School have a great favor to ask of you, but we hope it may be pleasant for you to grant it. We have an opportunity to spend a week end in the Poconos if properly chaperoned. We all thought of you immediately because we have enjoyed your company so much on former occasions, and because we know you like sports so much yourself. Two of us were there last year, and let me tempt you with some of the attractive high spots of our week end. To greet us, there was always a crackling wood fire in the enormous fireplace at the lodge—great logs burning. There was skiing and skating, and over the ice we took long rides on the dog sleds—beautiful fellows they were that pulled those sleds—Alaskan huskies. Every afternoon tea was served in front of the fire; in the evening there was dancing and ping-pong. If we wanted to be out-of-doors again in the evening, flood lights were thrown on the toboggan slides. Incidentally, the food was good.

I do hope I may hear from you soon saying that we may have the pleasure of meeting you Friday noon, the sixteenth of February.

Very sincerely yours,

Ann

Shrub Oak School
January 20

Request for Information

If a person wants an immediate reply to some request, he will write a rather brief letter, containing merely the request and a pleasant greeting.

Hillside School

Brewster, N. Y.

March 27, 19——

Dear Aunt Tat,

Will you help a fellow out of difficulties? I've been appointed chairman of the decorations for a matinee dance in May we seniors are giving the "Mollies" of Shrub Oak. That's short for girls of Saint Mary's Hall. We've had a boat, a Dutch garden, a ski train, a Chinese tea house, Tahiti, and goodness knows what else. You've never let me down before. Do come forward with something handsome and practical.

Mother writes that everything at our house is going on as usual. I hope you and Uncle Bob will be going over in two weeks when I have Saturday and Sunday at home.

Your loving nephew,

Dale

The reply will also be limited to the answering of the question. The writer has thus proved he has given his mind wholly to the request.

Confirmation

516 Forest Avenue
Oak Park, Illinois
February 1, 19——

My dear Peter,

When I had the pleasure of a brief chat with your father last week, he told me among other things that you are looking forward to being confirmed this spring when Bishop —— makes his annual visit at Saint Michael's Church. I congratulate you, Peter, on your decision. Your father and I were confirmed in the same class, years ago, and we later stood together with you at the baptismal font. You were quite small at the time. I am sending you a copy of "The Book of Common Prayer." Undoubtedly Christianity has been the greatest moving force for good the world has ever known. We have skyscrapers and bomber planes, but the ancient Egyptians had huge pyramids and the Assyrians horrible devices for waging war, so perhaps we haven't progressed so far in inventions; but have you ever been on a city street where a man, perhaps a beggar, was knocked down by an auto? Have you heard the policeman's whistle blown instantly, seen an ambulance drive up, attendants with a stretcher get out and take the injured man in a jiffy to the nearest hospital where he will receive the same medical care that his rich neighbor has? That, Peter, is one result of Christian doctrine. Get behind the movement and keep it going strong in your generation.

I hope it will be possible for me to accept your mother and father's invitation and come to Delevan in April.

Kindest regards to all your family.

Very truly yours,
Charles Sears

Request for Money

Riverview School
La Crosse, Wisconsin
December 10, 19——

Dear Mother,

This seems to be the season of the year when we remember all with gifts. We have one for the head of the school, for our class advisor, for the chaplain, for all the maids, for the janitor, for the offering in chapel, and then there are ones for the girls here in school. I've seen a few accessories I rather need for my dress for the dance, and as you may have guessed, I have but two dollars left from my allowance. How am I to plan for all these expenses? Is it a good thing to borrow on my future allowance, can I look for a bonus at Christmas because of good marks in exams, or do I just out and out ask for help? Can you send some sort of relief to your impoverished

Barbara

School Matters

RIVERVIEW SCHOOL
LA CROSSE, WISCONSIN

January 15, 19——

Dearest Mother,

Miss Lawrence will write you about my work, I'm sure. I hope it won't be too much of a shock to you, but I don't make any progress, and there isn't any use spending Dad's money to keep me here. I can't keep track of Caesar's daily marches. There is another pet pastime they have here, and that's finding what x equals. You know, I don't care at all; it can equal any old thing it wants to. I wonder if x cares. I generally try to accommodate and put down something, but it's usually wrong. Then all the fun the girls enjoy is chasing a ball of some kind around, and what the sense is in putting a ball inside a hoop, or over a net, or between posts, I don't see. Miss Lawrence was most understanding. She knows I like to care for little children, and she told me about a school where I can take courses about care of children, cooking, sociology, go on with biology, take applied arithmetic, and story telling. I'm a flop at this, but I'm sure I shouldn't be at that. I could start second semester if you'll let me. When I get through I could work in the nursery school division of some settlement, or I could even be a governess for small children. Maybe I'd learn how to keep house. I'd like very much to try. Do you want me to take the exams? I got 26 on my last algebra test.

Oh, Mother, this is awful. Do save me! I love you and Dad very much.

Devotedly,
Althea

MRS. THOMAS K. MUNSEN
FRONTENAC, MINNESOTA

January 15, 19——

Darling,

Your letter and one from Miss Lawrence came in the same mail. You seem to have had a very practical talk together, arriving at the conclusion that a course in home making and applied art would be beneficial for you. Daddy and I drove over to Red Wing last evening to see the school Miss Lawrence mentioned and to interview Miss Taylor. In the art room, we saw the weaving that girls had been doing and stencils for decoration on a nursery wall. The kitchen is a busy place during class hours. One class had served a luncheon for eight guests yesterday. There is a lovely sunny nursery and a small playground for the little tots that come during the day. Miss Taylor says she has placed several girls as assistants in social centers. We liked the girls we met, Cissy Newsom, especially. I wonder if you will!

You ask about your examinations. Yes, take them, by all means. You always want to finish what you start just as well as you can. If you had 26 on your last algebra test, perhaps you can make 36 this time. Try your best—you might surprise yourself, you know.

Lovingly,
Mother

61 Mill Lane
Delevan, Wisconsin
March 14, 19——

Mrs. John Cummings
Librarian, Delevan High School
City

My dear Mrs. Cummings,

Our dramatic society has decided to use the proceeds from the junior play this year to buy books for the library. We should like to make a few suggestions about purchases, subject, of course, to your approval. As we all study English history the second semester of our junior year as a background for English literature in the senior year, don't you think it advisable to increase the number of reference books in that section of the library? We should like to see the following books on our shelves:

Larson, L. M.: A History of England
Milne, A. A.: The Dover Road   Poems
Quennell, Marjorie and C. H. B.: Everyday Things in
   England
Strachey, L.: Eminent Victorians
Traill, H. D. (Editor): Social England

For records, we should like to suggest:

Siegfried's Rhine Journey—Wagner
The Ride of the Valkyries—Wagner (11614—$1.00)
The Water Music—Handel

We have liked the illustrations in Quennell and Traill, the biography of Gordon, especially, in "Eminent Victorians," the recent history in Prof. Larson's text, and we enjoyed group reading of "Changing Guard at Buckingham Palace" and "The King's Breakfast" by Milne. The Water Music was written for the King's barge on the Thames and while Wagner's subjects were not English, we have found so many references to Siegfried and the Valkyries, we should enjoy having the records.

We hope that you and the whole school will find pleasure in our gift.

Most sincerely yours,
Cora Strong
Secretary of the Dramatic Society

The Soldier

Soldiers like to hear all the gossip of the home town. They want to feel they are still remembered as part of the activities they left. Keep the letters bright and cheerful.

U. S. Naval Air Station
Kodiak, Alaska
December 8, 19———

Dear Aunt Janet,

Your last letter came on the boat a few days ago. I was glad to get the news of all the family, and hope that Ruth is herself again after her operation.

Christmas is really upon us here. It is entrancingly beautiful with the snow a foot deep all around, with the mountains sternly set in an austere blue sky, the lakes like cut glass, and the sea as green as a cat's eye. Although conditions are far from wonderful or even good, the beauty of the place makes it hard to dislike any part of it.

I should like a French grammar and dictionary. Several of us have been making noble attempts to expand our humble knowledge of the language, but the lack of a grammar naturally limits our efforts. As you asked what I'd like, I should appreciate it very much if you would send me a copy of each that you may have at home.

Thank you so much for your letter, and a very Merry Christmas and Happy New Year to you and all the family.

Sincerely,
Bart

Delevan, Wisconsin
January 27, 19——

Dear Bart,

Your aunt showed me the letter you wrote before Christmas. You must be seeing the world, and I think in congenial company. Three boys from here started off this week. Tom Nethercut, Bill Bergdahl, and Gene Baker are at Great Lakes now, entered to study in the navy machine shops. Tom wants to work on a ship's paper; he's had a good deal of training in printing in manual classes.

The town is on its toes in basketball. Our squad has won from Elkhart, Janeston, Whiteriver, and Sugar Creek. There's Richearth still to encounter and two return games; but if we ever had a look-in at the championship, it's right now. At the Whiteriver spring tournament the end of next month, we ought to show up pretty well. Paul Grant and Olaf Helgesen are the stars. Olaf holds top honors in points scored in the Southeastern Six so far. The townspeople are turning out in crowds for every game.

We're having rather warm weather for this season. The Wells company has had to call its trucks off the ice. It's too dangerous to cut now. The men are coming in from their huts built over the holes to fish. At night, the sound of the cracks widening is weird at this time of year. Naturally no skiing, no skating. But then, we go to the Armory for roller skating. You would enjoy some of the couples that are pairing off this winter—Bill has followed Hannah persistently for six weeks, Ardiss has finally corralled Bob, and the Bascom twins have definitely settled down to the inseparables, Gretchen and Patty.

For town news, apply to old Ed Staver. He's undertaken to direct the Boy Scouts in collecting paper. His duties take him so much among us, he's known now as the ubiquitous Ed. He helps Miss Cornelia with the new heater she installed in the chicken house, for the sake of getting all those old papers she has hoarded in her basement; he helped Mrs. Trinket clean Judge Sloan's office and received about half a ton of Congressional records along with his pay. I'd say he's doing his bit.

We expect to hear Mr. Cuthbert from Milwaukee tell of his experiences in France and England. He's a cousin of our new rector who has induced him to come to Delevan. There will be defense stamps handy to buy. Our Red Cross quota has been oversubscribed. All the little towns are working away. We miss you and your "saxe," but we'll do our best to keep you tooting it under as good conditions as possible.

As ever,
Don